ROMANS
AND
GALATIANS
A Devotional Commentary

ROMANS
AND GALATIANS

A Devotional Commentary

Meditations on St. Paul's

Letter to the Romans

and

Letter to the Galatians

GENERAL EDITOR

Leo Zanchettin

The Word Among Us Press
9639 Doctor Perry Road
Ijamsville, Maryland 21754
www.wau.org
ISBN: 0-932085-70-9

Scripture quotations are from the Revised Standard Version of the Bible, © 1946, 1952, 1971, by the Division of Christian Education of the National Council of the Churches of Christ in the U.S.A. Used by permission.

Cover Art:
Portrait of St. Paul, by Pompeo Batoni
National Trust/Art Resource, NY

Cover design by Christopher Ranck

Made and printed in the United States of America.

Foreword

Dear Friends in Christ:

If someone were to come up to you on a street corner or in the market and ask you to explain the gospel, what would you say? How much time would you need to find the right words that conveyed both your personal story and deep theological doctrines like sin, redemption, or salvation? How confident would you be that you have fully explained what it means to believe in Jesus Christ?

These were probably some of the thoughts in St. Paul's mind as he sat down to write a letter introducing himself and his message to the Christian church in Rome. He had wanted Rome to be his new base of operations, so he sought to put the believers there at ease about who he was and what he taught. These questions were probably in his mind for different reasons when he received news that many people in the church in Galatia were beginning to abandon the simplicity of the gospel for a more complex and elitist version preached by some of his enemies. Paul knew he needed to intervene—and strongly—to keep the Galatian Christians from losing the freedom and joy they knew when they first accepted Christ.

Given the situations in which they were written, it's no wonder that both letters have very strong reputations. Romans is generally considered Paul's theological masterpiece, and Galatians is seen as perhaps the most personal and fiery letter of his that has come down to us. And in a way, it's appropriate that both letters would often be linked, as they are in this commentary. In both letters, Paul tackles the question of salvation through faith in Christ. In both letters he explains the relationship between the Jewish law and the new covenant in Christ. And finally, in both letters Paul speaks with great passion about the way the Holy Spirit wants to work in our hearts.

Perhaps the most powerful tie is the fact that in both letters Paul practically sings and shouts aloud the message of freedom that is at the heart of the gospel. Because of Jesus' death and resurrection, we have been released from sin! Where sin abounded, grace abounded even more (Romans 5:20)! We have been crucified with Christ! Jesus Christ himself actually lives within us (Galatians 2:20)! Nothing—nothing at all—can separate us from the love of God that is in Christ Jesus our Lord (Romans 8:39)! In verse after verse, Paul explains, rejoices in, and illustrates the liberation from sin that is the heritage of every baptized believer. This liberation is so much more than release from the weight of sin. It's the freedom not only to walk away from sin, but also to walk boldly and confidently into the throne room of God and talk to him as "Abba," our heavenly yet intimate Father who will never abandon us (Romans 8:15; Galatians 4:6).

This message of freedom is at the heart of this devotional commentary on Romans and Galatians. Our goal is to offer meditations on every passage in these letters—meditations which we hope will bring you to a deeper experience of the freedom Paul knew and described so passionately. We know that the more time we spend prayerfully contemplating Scripture, the more opportunity we give the Lord to speak to us personally, and in so speaking, to change our hearts. As we pray through these powerful letters, may we all come to cry out with Paul: "For freedom Christ has set us free!" (Galatians 5:1).

We want to thank everyone who has made this commentary possible, especially all of the writers who contributed meditations. Some of the meditations appearing in this book were initially developed for *The Word Among Us* monthly publication, and we are grateful to these writers for granting us permission to reprint their work. We also want to thank Fr. Joseph Mindling, O.F.M. Cap., and Fr. Joseph Wimmer, O.S.A., for contributing the introductory chapters, as well as Ann Bottenhorn for her considerable contributions to the meditations. Finally, we want to thank Jeanne Kun, without whose tireless work and numerous contributions on so many levels this book would not have been possible at all. May the Lord abundantly bless each of them!

Leo Zanchettin
General Editor

Table of Contents

Messages of Faith, Freedom, and Salvation

An Introduction to St. Paul's Letters to the Romans and Galatians

By Fr. Joseph A. Mindling, O.F.M. Cap.

The letters to the Romans and the Galatians are among the most frequently quoted, the most thought-provoking, and the most spiritually uplifting compositions in the New Testament. Nevertheless, they are writings preserved from a time and a culture significantly different from our own. Because of these differences, it's helpful to look at the main teachings of these letters in light of their historical context. That way, we can begin to see how Paul's words here applied both to his readers back then and to us today.

The author of both these sacred letters, Paul of Tarsus, was born into a strict Pharisaic family, who sent him to Jerusalem for rabbinical studies. There, as a young adult, he involved himself zealously in the attempt to stamp out the Christian movement in its earliest days. However, a personal encounter with the risen Christ converted Paul into a tireless advocate of the same religion he had once persecuted. From that point on, although he always tried to maintain connections with his Jewish brothers and sisters, Paul began to "specialize" in spreading Christianity among the primarily gentile peoples who lived outside the Holy Land.

Many episodes of Paul's life as a missionary are reflected in the Acts of the Apostles, but reading Paul's letters can offer us an even more direct contact with his spirit and thought. Paul's relationship with the original recipients of all the New Testament letters that bear his name was based in their shared relationship with Jesus. Still, he had a different personal history with each group, a history which significantly influenced the way he wrote to each of them.

Romans: An Introduction and an Appeal. Although none of the writings of the New Testament states when it was written, internal clues lead scholars to estimate that Paul wrote his letter to the Romans shortly before his final visit to Jerusalem in the late 50s. Before writing this richly theological and pastoral letter to the believers in Rome, Paul had evangelized in the areas that would correspond to present-day Syria, Turkey, and Greece. However, he had apparently never visited the capital city of the empire and the cultural and business center of the Mediterranean world.

No records of the actual founding of the church in Rome have survived, but it is clear that the majority of its members—some converts from Judaism and many others from various pagan religions—owed their exposure to the gospel to preachers other than Paul. Nevertheless, the large number of personal greetings to individuals whose names he mentions at the end of his letter indicates that this widely traveled missionary had more than enough contacts to keep him in touch with important developments in the church there.

At the time when Paul wrote this letter, he was preparing to spend some time in Rome, passing through on his way to new missionary territory in Spain. One important purpose for writing was to present himself as both a knowledgeable thinker and a competent pastor, for he hoped to win the Romans' support for his new mission. At the same time, Paul appreciated the chance to interact with and benefit from contact with these believers, whose faith had become "common knowledge throughout the empire" (1:8-13).* As a first step toward both these goals,

---

* The author's own paraphrase of Scripture texts is used here and throughout this chapter.

Paul wrote this letter, which took the form of a methodical presentation of his understanding of God's plan of salvation.

What Is the Gospel Message? After a brief but impressive self-introduction (1:1-16), Paul begins by reflecting on the way human history has continually spiraled into a moral decline from which we simply cannot free ourselves. He identifies the root cause of this deterioration in the sinful refusal, of Gentiles and Jews alike, to accept God and his authority over all creation—not just a recognition in words, but an acknowledgment demonstrated in consistent religious obedience (1:17–3:20).

Despite our past acts of disobedience, though, our future destiny is far from hopeless. Even though no human initiative could reverse the consequences of sin that began with Adam, God himself offers us a way out. If we accept his invitation to trust Jesus as a new Adam, with a faith that opens us to the transforming power of his death and resurrection, our relationship with God can be reestablished. Paul calls this readmission to God's good graces "justification," a word which in its original literal sense meant a "straightening out" or a "making right again" (3:21–5:21).

Baptism is the gateway into this new relationship, yet incorporation into Christ does not separate us from temptation and human weakness. As long as we live, we are at risk of sinning and losing God's friendship again. What baptism does give us, however, is the indwelling of the Holy Spirit, who comes to strengthen us and direct us. Instead of helpless frustration over our inability to grasp and carry out God's will, faith gives us access to the hope and the strength we need to regain and remain in his favor (6:1–8:39).

All of this is deeply reassuring for those who have become united with Christ through faith and baptism, but what about the Jewish people who have rejected the gospel? Concerned and saddened by this situation, Paul attributes their resistance both to human stubbornness and, paradoxically, to a divine "hardening of hearts." At the same time, however, he is confident that all of Israel will eventually be saved, as a fulfillment of God's irrevocable promises. Moreover, Paul is certain that God's providence is actually finessing their present refusal into an offer of "most favored" status to everyone without distinction (9:1–11:36).

The transformation of the older covenant relationship with God that Jesus' life, death, and resurrection have brought about requires, in turn, a transformation in the way people of faith should think and act. To make this concrete, Paul brings his letter to a climax with a variety of moral exhortations which illustrate several practical aspects of our life in grace—whether we act individually or collectively as members of the Body of Christ (12:1–16:27).

Galatians: A Passionate Defense of the Gospel. Unlike the situation in more cosmopolitan Rome, the churches in Galatia were predominantly rural congregations, and it was Paul's own preaching and example that had attracted them from idolatry to faith in Christ. Much to his disgruntlement, Paul discovered that sometime after his most recent visit (sometime in the 50s), certain self-appointed agitators from Jerusalem had infiltrated these outlying communities and convinced a significant number of them that the gospel they had received from Paul was misleading and inadequate.

Insidiously passing themselves off as representatives from Jerusalem, the mother church, these "false brothers" insisted that gentile converts had to fulfill more religious obligations than Paul had required of them. These included circumcision, obeying dietary restrictions, and following rabbinical liturgical calendars. Paul uses the term "the law" to refer to this approach—characteristic of first-century Judaism—which put such arbitrary and symbolic traditions on a par with the two fundamental commandments: love of God and love of neighbor. Together with other early Christian leaders, Paul was convinced that such additions were no longer binding under the new covenant.

Angered by the way these false brothers had maligned him, and moved by a deep pastoral concern for his Galatian "children" and "brothers" (4:12,19; 5:11; 6:18), Paul reacted with indignation. He realized from his personal experience with these beloved but less sophisticated communities that he needed to address them with blunt but convincing clarity if he wanted to squelch the intruders and counteract the effects of their false teachings.

Justification, Faith, and Freedom. After a brief, somewhat formal opening, Paul moves immediately into a scathing condemnation of those who had dared to misrepresent what he taught. He then issues a series of stern rebukes against those Galatians who allowed themselves to be swayed from the authentic gospel of Christ (1:1-10). Paul reminds them that his initial coming to proclaim the good news had been prompted by a personal commissioning from the risen Lord and that he had also received the explicit approval of the church leaders in Jerusalem. In fact, he even cites an instance where he challenged Peter, a recognized "pillar" of the church, for contributing earlier to a breakdown in the full social integration of converts from Hebrew and gentile backgrounds up in Antioch (1:11–2:14).

Having demonstrated the unassailable basis for his apostolic authority, Paul next moves into a fivefold defense of his pivotal teaching that "man is not justified by legal observance but by faith in Jesus Christ." Justification, in turn, results in inner transformation: "I have been crucified with Christ, and the life I live now is not my own: Christ is living in me" (2:16,20).

1. *The Spirit.* Paul's first argument is a rather caustic appeal to the personal experience of the presence and the wondrous power of the Spirit in their own lives: "You foolish Galatians! How did you receive the Spirit? Was it through observance of the law or through faith in what you heard?" (3:1-5).

2. *Faith and the Law.* The second line of defense is based on Hebrew Scripture. True to his rabbinical training, Paul combines Habakkuk 2:4, which declares that "the just man shall live by faith," with Genesis 15:6, which says that "Abraham believed God and it was credited to him as justice." Then he brings in Exodus 12:40, which states that the Law of Moses was given centuries after Abraham's day. Thus Paul depicts the father of the chosen people as a perfect model of the gospel he had preached to the Galatians.

Since the law could not empower anyone to comply with its prescriptions, Paul sees that insisting on this antiquated "training program" would amount to turning a useful, but temporary, blessing into a kind of curse. What really counts is not genealogy, gender, or social status, but a *trust* that bonds us through the crucified Christ with God's true children in the faith of Abraham: "If you belong to Christ then you are Abraham's seed, heirs according to the promise" (3:6-29).

3. *No Longer a Slave, But an Heir.* The third image Paul uses against his opponents is an appeal to the Galatians' natural desire to consider themselves as spiritually mature and free. He describes their earlier situation as idolaters as a kind of slavery to elements of the created world. Just as they would not want to revert to their former slavery, he urges them not to submit to the law. To do so would be to become "minors" once again, no better than slaves or children who have not yet achieved the full liberty of adult heirs (4:1-11).

4. *"Become As I Am."* Paul's fourth defense is based on an attempt to touch his readers psychologically. He reminds them of the original caring and trusting relationship they shared with him—a friendship which was instrumental in their receiving the gospel. By contrast, he accuses his opponents of being motivated by a base desire for praise: "They want to exclude you so that you may make much of them" (4:12-20).

5. *Children of the Promise*. Paul's final argument takes the form of a scriptural allegory about the two sons of Abraham: Ishmael (portrayed as an oppressor), and Isaac, the son of Sarah (who symbolizes the ideal Jerusalem). Despite his biological (and earlier) relationship with his father, Ishmael was rejected, while Isaac inherited everything because he carried forward the heritage of Abraham's faith. Thus, the Galatians' faith in Jesus, *the* "Seed of Abraham," makes them more authentically children of the promise than Paul's opponents, who may be physically related to Abraham but who rely in vain on compliance with the externals of the law to save them (4:21-31).

Being Transformed through Faith. Paul devotes most of the last two chapters of his letter to addressing some of the practical ramifications of what he taught in the earlier sections. Apparently, rumors had been circulated suggesting that he might actually make some exceptions to his teaching about freedom from the law. Paul denounces this absolutely as a "bodily" way of thinking, which must be crucified and replaced by a carefully fostered life of freedom in the Spirit.

To illustrate what he meant by "works of the law of the flesh" Paul offers a broad sampling of sinful activities which must be shunned, including not just sexual misconduct but more than a dozen examples of immoral excesses which sound as familiar to us today as they would have to the original readers of this letter. He next balances these by itemizing an even more extensive list of virtues that demonstrate the presence of the Spirit helping us to implement "the law of Christ" (6:2).

The final verses of chapter 6 are constituted primarily by parting shots against not only the teachings but also the motives of the opponents who had triggered, like grains of sand in an oyster, the pearls of thought in this lively letter. And in one final autobiographical stroke, Paul leaves all of us with an image of himself: not a peevish but a fiercely protective pastor, carrying the marks of Jesus branded on his body.

Harvesting the Spiritual Treasures of These Epistles. It would certainly be possible to approach Romans and Galatians as interesting pieces of ancient literature, or to look at them just as we might look at specimens in a glass museum case. However, for readers who confidently approach these letters as vessels of God's revelation, they come alive with consolation, challenge, and insight.

Introductions such as this one and other sources of background information can help us read these sacred texts with greater understanding. Nevertheless, the most important tools we can ever bring to our reading or hearing of the Scriptures are a desire to absorb whatever God has in store for us, and a determination to listen attentively to every detail with the ears of a docile faith.

Paul of Tarsus

A Life of St. Paul

By Fr. Joseph F. Wimmer, O.S.A.

The story and legacy of St. Paul loom so large, both in the New Testament and in the history of the church, that we can sometimes lose sight of the man in the midst of the story. Even Paul's most famous moment—his sudden conversion to Christianity—is wrapped in mystery. Writing about it himself, Paul simply says:

> I persecuted the church of God violently and tried to destroy it; and I advanced in Judaism beyond many of my own age among my people, so extremely zealous was I for the traditions of my fathers. But . . .[God] who had set me apart before I was born, and had called me through his grace, was pleased to reveal his Son to me, in order that I might preach him among the Gentiles. (Galatians 1:13-16)

Luke describes Paul's conversion three times (Acts 9:1-19; 22:3-16; and 26:2-18), but is vague about some of the details: What, for example, was seen or heard, and by whom (compare Acts 9:7 with 22:9)? Paul emphasizes the certainty of his conversion, and Luke emphasizes its suddenness. Perhaps we may conjecture that as Paul was making the 150-mile journey from Jerusalem to Damascus on his donkey, he was coming to grips with the difference between the simplicity, honesty, and courage of the Christians, and the narrow-minded hardness of himself. Could it be that Paul was on the wrong side? And what about the view of the revered Gamaliel, that if the Christian movement came from God, no one could stop it?

However it happened, Jesus' sudden appearance to him, of which Paul is utterly certain (1 Corinthians 9:1; 15:3-8), was an overwhelming experience that changed his life forever. The fierce persecutor of the Christians was now one of its most zealous preachers, an irony that both Luke (Acts 9:20-22) and even Paul himself (Galatians 1:23; 1 Corinthians 15:9-10) noticed. That event set Paul on a path that would take him through much of the civilized world, embroil him in theological and even political debates, and place him in harm's way on a seemingly regular basis. But through it all, Paul remained unswervingly committed to Christ, the one who appeared to him in glory on the Damascus road.

Paul the Pharisee. What had driven Paul to try almost single-handedly to destroy this new Christian movement? Part of the motivation must have been his feeling that it was undermining his beloved Jewish faith. In his letter to the Philippians, Paul had described himself as "a Hebrew born of Hebrews; as to the law a Pharisee . . . as to righteousness under the law blameless" (Philippians 3:5-6).

"Blameless!" Paul had wanted to carry out the prescriptions of the Torah perfectly. That was why he had joined the Pharisaic movement. The Pharisees were laymen who had banded together sometime after the Exile into *havurot*, or groups of "table fellowship," in order to keep the precepts of the law totally by mutual support. In their observance, they went beyond the precepts of the laws, setting a "fence" around it in order to avoid the very possibility of breaking a rule. Love for God and fidelity to his law was their ideal. Unfortunately, such concern for perfect observance could lead to pride, disdain for others, and focus on externals. It took Paul some extraordinary experiences to learn this lesson. But his love for God never diminished.

It is not clear whether Paul ever met the earthly Jesus. The Second Letter to the Corinthians (5:16) hints that he did, but did not appreciate who Jesus really was. As a Pharisee, Paul would have been bitterly opposed to the abrogations of the Torah that characterized Jesus' teaching: consorting with outcasts and sinners, relativizing the importance of purity laws and of the Sabbath, overturning Moses' commands concerning divorce and taking oaths. Paul's wrath was all the greater against the first Christians, since they were damaging the unity of the Jewish community by their divergent teachings and by the high place which they accorded to Jesus as Messiah, Son of God, and risen Lord. Paul took the initiative against them in Jerusalem, assisted in the stoning of the deacon Stephen (Acts 7:58–8:3), and asked the high priest for authorization to persecute Christians even as far as Damascus (9:1-2).

Paul the Roman Citizen. Yet there was another side to Paul. He was not only Jewish; he was also Greek. It's not true that after his conversion he changed his name from Saul to Paul so as to be more acceptable to the Gentiles to whom he would preach. He grew up with two names—the Hebrew "Saul," and the Greek "Paul"—as did many other Jews in the Diaspora of that time.

Paul was born about 10 A.D. in Cilicia, Asia Minor, the farthest eastern corner of the Roman Empire (eastern Turkey today), in the port city of Tarsus. Alexander the Great had conquered it in 334 B.C. and made it a Hellenistic city. Cicero had been governor there in 51 B.C., and Antony had declared Tarsus a "free city" around 42 B.C., with power to mint its own coins and be exempt from export-import taxes.

Paul was justly proud of his city and of his Roman citizenship (Acts 21:39; 22:25-29). He probably went to a Greek-speaking school in Tarsus during his early years. His knowledge of the Greek language and culture enabled him to travel the whole Mediterranean basin with ease and to address thousands of Gentiles with great success. In his writings Paul often quotes the Old Testament from memory in its Greek translation, the Septuagint, but he also knows the Hebrew text, which he sometimes prefers to the Greek. Clearly, he was well versed in both languages and could live in both the Hebrew and the Greek world with no problem (22:2).

Paul the Christian Neophyte. Upon his dramatic conversion, Paul was baptized in Damascus and immediately began preaching his new faith there, that Jesus was the Messiah (Acts 9:18-22). Luke writes that "when many days had passed," the Jews in Damascus conspired to kill Paul, but he was lowered over the wall at night in a basket and escaped to Jerusalem (9:23-25). Paul remembers the incident well, and even notes that it was the governor of Damascus under King Aretas who was seeking his capture (2 Corinthians 11:32-33). This would have happened around 38 or 39 A.D., since King Aretas died in 39 or 40 A.D., "three years" after Paul's conversion, which would have taken place around 35 or 36 A.D. (Galatians 1:17-18).

Paul went to Jerusalem, where he debated the Hellenistic Jews—probably his former comrades. He so incensed them, however, that they tried to kill him as an apostate (Acts 9:24-29). Paul escaped again, this time to the port of Caesarea on the Mediterranean, and returned by ship to his hometown of Tarsus (Acts 9:30; Galatians 1:21). He remained there for five or six years (38 or 39-44 A.D.).

Luke is silent on how Paul spent his time in Tarsus, but Paul himself tells us that he was preaching "in the regions of Syria and Cilicia" (Galatians 1:21). We may suppose he was growing daily in the faith and in knowledge about the mystery of Jesus. This Galilean rabbi really was the crucified but risen Messiah, the Son of God sent by the Father to bring salvation not only to the Jews, but also to Gentiles. What's more, Jesus would return soon to judge the whole world on the Day of the Lord.

Above all, Paul learned that salvation is a free gift of God through the life, death, and resurrection of Jesus. All we need to do is accept it with a faith "active in good works" (1 Thessalonians 1:3; Galatians 5:6). These are major themes that appear again and again, beginning with Paul's earliest extant epistle, the First Letter to the Thessalonians (51 A.D.). In his zeal Paul needed to share his faith with everyone around him, gaining new insights in the very process of debate.

These were happy years that led to profound depths of prayer. Much later, around 57 A.D., Paul still remembers fondly this period of "visions and revelations of the Lord." He says, "I know a man in Christ who fourteen years ago [around 43 A.D., during this time of quiet preparation for his ministry] was caught up to the third heaven—whether in the body or out of the body I do not know, God knows—and he heard things that cannot be told, which man may not utter" (2 Corinthians 12:2-4). That mystical experience of Christ remained constantly with Paul: "It is no longer I who live, but Christ who lives in me" (Galatians 2:20); "For to me to live is Christ, and to die is gain" (Philippians 1:21).

The Journeys Begin. Around 44 A.D. the apostle Barnabas came to Tarsus to invite Paul to join him in Syrian Antioch, an important Greco-Roman city where Christians were gathering in great numbers. Paul remained there at least a year (Acts 11:26), after which he began what Luke describes as his "first missionary journey." After going to Judea in order to bring famine relief to the elders there (11:27-30), Paul and Barnabas went on about a three-year tour to preach the gospel (46-49 A.D.). They evangelized the island of Cyprus, then continued by boat to the southern coast of Asia Minor, where they spent most of the next two years. Paul usually began by preaching Christ in the synagogue of a particular city. But when rebuffed, he turned to the Gentiles, who were often more receptive. According to Luke's account of his sermon in Antioch of Pisidia (13:13-43), Paul began his preaching with a brief history of the major stages of the Old Testament, focused on the messianic promises made by the prophets, and showed how they were fulfilled in Jesus, who was put to death but raised by God and appeared to many, bringing them forgiveness of sin and the promise of eternal life.

After their return to Antioch, Paul and Barnabas set out again, this time for the famous Council of Jerusalem (49 A.D.), to decide whether or not potential Christians must first be circumcised and be held to observation of the laws of Judaism. Paul tells us how he argued against the need for circumcision and won the day. He was asked only to care for the poor, which he was happy to do (Galatians 2:1-10). Luke also mentions some further obligations, such as abstaining from blood, strangled meat or meat offered to idols, and fornication (Acts 15:29). Paul found out about these additions later when he visited James in Jerusalem (21:25). Apparently Paul had left for Antioch before the council was concluded.

The Second Missionary Journey: Into Greece. In all these travels, Paul had not yet entered Greece, but his "second missionary journey" (Acts 15:40–18:22) was to change that. During the years 50-52 A.D., Paul and Silas (also known as Silvanus) preached throughout Syria and central Asia Minor, where they met Timothy, who joined them. These friendships were very important to Paul, and he mentions them in the opening of several of his letters (1 and 2 Thessalonians; 2 Corinthians; Philippians; and Philemon). At the port city of Troas on the western coast of Asia Minor, Luke joined them, and at the urging of the Holy Spirit all four crossed the Aegean Sea and headed into Europe (Acts 16:9-12). They came eventually to Philippi, a Roman colony in northern Greece, where a wealthy woman named Lydia took them into her home. Because of Jewish opposition in Philippi, Paul and Silas were imprisoned there, but they were delivered through an earthquake and continued overland to another

Macedonian port, Thessalonica. As usual, Paul taught in the synagogue that Jesus the Messiah had to suffer, die, and rise again (17:3). Along with Philippi, Thessalonica always remained dear to Paul's heart. He exhorted the believers there to be faithful, for "you are our glory and joy" (1 Thessalonians 2:20), just as he reminded the Philippians that they were his "joy and crown" (Philippians 4:1).

At Athens, Paul's next major stop, he saw statues and altars to many gods, even one "to the unknown god." Paul used the occasion to preach his famous sermon "On the Unknown God" (Acts 17:22-31). Quoting Greek authors, he told how the Greeks themselves admitted that God was not far away but near, for "in him we live and move and are" (Epimenides of Knossos), and indeed, "we too are his offspring" (Aratus of Soli; Acts 17:28). He then explained how God was now calling for repentance in preparation for the divine judgment on the last day. This was the very reason why God had raised Jesus from the dead, Paul explained. When they heard about the resurrection, many of the Athenians scoffed. They believed in the immortality of the soul, but could not see that a resurrected body would be of any use in the next world. Still, some did believe and accept baptism.

From Athens, Paul continued on to Corinth. There he met fellow tentmakers, Aquila and his wife Priscilla, both of whom had been expelled from Rome by Emperor Claudius around 40 A.D., and who became Paul's close friends and coworkers. Their ministry in Corinth was so successful that Paul remained one-and-a-half years (Acts 18:11), and wrote his first letter to the Thessalonians from there (1 Thessalonians 3:1,6). He also had opponents, and was brought by some of them to the tribunal of the proconsul Gallio in 52 A.D. Gallio, however, refused to accept the case and let Paul go free (Acts 18:12-17). Paul next sailed for Ephesus with Aquila and Priscilla, left them there (18:19) and continued home to Antioch (18:22).

The Third Missionary Journey and the Voyage Home. During his "third missionary journey" (Acts 18:23–21:17), between the years 54-58 A.D., Paul spent three months in Ephesus. Again, trouble erupted when the silversmiths there rioted against him. Evidently, they were losing a lot of business because the demand for their statues of Artemis, the "Queen of the Ephesians," had diminished as so many people abandoned the gods of the Greeks and embraced Jesus instead.

Paul was spared any violence when the riot was broken up, and he next moved on to Greece, where he spent about half a year strengthening the communities there before beginning his journey home. This would be his last trip, and his stops along the way were tinged with the sadness of parting but also with the beauty of friendship, of eucharistic meals, and of final exhortations (Acts 20:6-12).

Paul was anxious to return to Jerusalem to celebrate Pentecost there, but the trip became increasingly poignant and ominous. When he arrived at Tyre, friends warned him not to go on to Jerusalem. Then at Caesarea four daughters of a deacon named Philip warned him about the dangers of Jerusalem, and Agabus, a respected elder in the church with the gift of prophecy, foretold trouble and even captivity for Paul. Still, he persisted, saying, "I am ready not only to be imprisoned but even to die at Jerusalem for the name of the Lord Jesus" (Acts 21:13).

The Final Years: Captivity, Rome, and Martyrdom. When Paul arrived at Jerusalem, he was received warmly by his friends, but some Jews recognized him in the temple, seized him, and tried to kill him. The Roman commander arrested Paul and gave him a chance to confront his accusers before the Jewish council. Paul told them that he was on trial because he was a Pharisee and because of the resurrection from the dead. This threw the group into a turmoil, for the Pharisees believed in resurrection from the dead, but the Sadducees—who made up most of the council—did not (Acts 21:17–23:10).

For his own safety, Paul was transferred to a Roman prison in Caesarea. A week later Ananias, the high priest, came to testify against him before Felix, the Roman governor. Felix, however, simply left Paul in prison for two years (58-60 A.D.), until his term as governor expired (Acts 24:27). His successor, Porcius Festus, tried to resolve the issue, but rather than return to Jerusalem, Paul took advantage of his Roman citizenship by appealing to Caesar (25:11). Instead of Jerusalem, he would go to Rome.

In the fall of 60 A.D. Paul embarked for Rome, but even this trip would prove to be adventurous. His ship was caught in a fierce storm, and the passengers and crew were shipwrecked on the island of Malta. While Paul spent three winter months there waiting for another ship, he took advantage of the situation to preach the gospel among the Maltese (Acts 26:32–28:11). In early 61 A.D. he reached Puteoli, near Naples, then traveled overland to Rome (28:11-16). Paul spent about two years there under house arrest (61-63 A.D.). Even so, he was able to proclaim "the kingdom of God" and to teach "about the Lord Jesus Christ" (28:31).

Luke ends his story at this point, for he was writing not a biography of Paul, but the history of the word of God preached from Jerusalem to the ends of the earth (Acts 1:8), of which Rome was the symbol. However, Eusebius and some other ancient writers claimed that Paul was released from prison, went west—possibly as far as Spain—and was imprisoned a second time in Rome, after which he was beheaded under Nero around 67 A.D.

Scholars are not so sure about this last part of the timeline, however. The Pastoral Epistles (1 and 2 Timothy; Titus) have been invoked as indications of Pauline activity after his imprisonment in Rome, but most exegetes feel that because of their language, style, and developed state of church organization, they were not written by Paul but by his disciples. It seems probable, then, that Paul was kept under house arrest in Rome until he was beheaded at the beginning of Nero's persecution of the Christians in 64 A.D. However he met his end, one thing is certain: As he had done for thirty years, even at the end Paul poured out his life for Jesus, who had so graciously called him and blessed him.

A Life of Love. In the Second Letter to the Corinthians, Paul lists his sufferings, both external and internal: "Five times I have received at the hands of the Jews the forty lashes less one. Three times I have been beaten with rods; once I was stoned. Three times I have been shipwrecked . . . apart from other things, there is the daily pressure upon me of my anxiety for all the churches" (2 Corinthians 11:24-25,28). Paul's missionary zeal for God and care for his flock never slackened. He led an intense and heroic life of dedication both to God and to his brothers and sisters. It was his way of embracing Christ who first embraced him (Philippians 3:12), of living a life of love.

The Just Judgment of God

ROMANS
1:1–3:20

Romans 1:1-7

[1]   Paul, a servant of Jesus Christ, called to be an apostle, set apart for the gospel of God [2] which he promised beforehand through his prophets in the holy scriptures, [3] the gospel concerning his Son, who was descended from David according to the flesh [4] and designated Son of God in power according to the Spirit of holiness by his resurrection from the dead, Jesus Christ our Lord, [5] through whom we have received grace and apostleship to bring about the obedience of faith for the sake of his name among all the nations, [6] including yourselves who are called to belong to Jesus Christ;

[7]   To all God's beloved in Rome, who are called to be saints:

Grace to you and peace from God our Father and the Lord Jesus Christ.

Paul was called by God to be an apostle—one who would carry the message of Christ *and* proclaim his presence beyond Palestine to the far reaches of the Roman world. Paul made it his life's work to demonstrate that the divine promises first made to the Jewish people were actually fulfilled in Jesus Christ.

Paul's clearest written expression of the good news as he proclaimed it appears in his letter to the Romans. The truths taught in this letter are not just important doctrines for theologians to ponder—these truths are meant to *change* the lives of all who read them. Paul's intent was that this letter, through the work of the Spirit, would lead to inner change in all who pondered it.

The good news recognizes that the promises made to Israel are fulfilled in Jesus Christ. We get a taste of this even in Paul's initial greetings to the Romans: Paul had become a "servant" who was "called" and "set apart" (Romans 1:1), just as Moses and Abraham had been called to serve Yahweh. The "gospel of God" which Paul was called to preach was not something newly devised, but something "promised beforehand through his prophets in the holy scriptures" (1:2).

Paul proclaimed Jesus "descended from David" (Romans 1:3), the fulfillment of Jewish messianic hope. He knew Jesus to be "Son of God" (1:4) by his resurrection from the dead. As descended from the flesh through David and declared Son of God by the Spirit, Jesus is Messiah, Savior, and Lord (1:4) for all—Jew *and* Gentile. The faith which Paul tried to bring about (1:5) is the same obedient faith God expected from his covenant people, Israel. Jesus came not to abolish the law and prophets, but to fulfill them (Matthew 5:17), which he did through an obedient heart within.

Paul concluded his greetings with a blessing: "Grace to you and peace from God our Father and the Lord Jesus Christ" (Romans 1:7). The "grace" to which the Gentiles are newly called is the experience of God's favor; it was joined with God's peace, the shalom God bestowed on his chosen people. To the Romans and to us, Paul prayed God's grace and peace, that the same God who lovingly and justly watched over the Jewish people throughout their history would give abundant blessing and peace in his Son, the Lord Jesus Christ.

Romans 1:8-15

⁸ First, I thank my God through Jesus Christ for all of you, because your faith is proclaimed in all the world. ⁹ For God is my witness, whom I serve with my spirit in the gospel of his Son, that without ceasing I mention you always in my prayers, ¹⁰ asking that somehow by God's will I may now at last succeed in coming to you. ¹¹ For I long to see you, that I may impart to you some spiritual gift to strengthen you, ¹² that is, that we may be mutually encouraged by each other's faith, both yours and mine. ¹³ I want you to know, brethren, that I have often intended to come to you (but thus far have been prevented), in order that I may reap some harvest among you as well as among the rest of the Gentiles. ¹⁴ I am under obligation both to Greeks and to barbarians, both to the wise and to the foolish: ¹⁵ so I am eager to preach the gospel to you also who are in Rome.

The community in Rome was not one that Paul had founded. In fact, he did not even know very many of the Roman Christians when he wrote them this letter, yet he already felt a deep affection for them. News of the depth of their faith—praised throughout the world—had filled him with thanks and praise to God, and now he was eager to visit them and see it in action for himself (Romans 1:8,10).

As he opened his letter to the Roman Christians, Paul told them that he was looking forward to reaping a harvest of some sort among them (Romans 1:13-15). Whether this meant new converts or a deepening of their own grasp of the gospel, we do not know. He did not, however, expect his visit to be one-sided. Paul knew that he would receive many blessings through his brothers and sisters in Rome, and he looked forward to enjoying their fellowship. Clearly this visit was an opportunity for himself and the Romans to "be mutually encouraged by each other's faith" (1:12) as the Holy Spirit knit them all more closely to one another.

Brothers and sisters in the Lord are a priceless treasure. Through our fellowship together, the Holy Spirit builds us. As we support one another and call one another on to greater hope and trust in God, our faith is strengthened. Just as Paul hoped to impart spiritual gifts to the Romans by his presence with them (Romans 1:11), we give— and receive—many spiritual gifts and blessings in our relationships with each other.

Treasure and deepen the Christian friendships you already have. Don't take your brothers and sisters in the Lord for granted or neglect them. But also allow the Holy Spirit to guide you and to open new doors for fellowship with others beyond your present circle. God is eager to bring his people together—in your parish or your prayer group, at your workplace, through sharing with Christians of other denominations in common efforts such as serving in a soup kitchen or shelter for the homeless, or by doing pro-life work.

Ask the Lord to give you a heart like Paul's—a heart full of thanks for everyone who is a part of your "family of faith" and a heart eager to reach out and proclaim the gospel so that many more may join that family!

Romans 1:16-32

16 For I am not ashamed of the gospel: it is the power of God for salvation to every one who has faith, to the Jew first and also to the Greek. 17 For in it the righteousness of God is revealed through faith for faith; as it is written, "He who through faith is righteous shall live."

18 For the wrath of God is revealed from heaven against all ungodliness and wickedness of men who by their wickedness suppress the truth. 19 For what can be known about God is plain to them, because God has shown it to them. 20 Ever since the creation of the world his invisible nature, namely, his eternal power and deity, has been clearly perceived in the things that have been made. So they are without excuse; 21 for although they knew God they did not honor him as God or give thanks to him, but they became futile in their thinking and their senseless minds were darkened. 22 Claiming to be wise, they became fools, 23 and exchanged the glory of the immortal God for images resembling mortal man or birds or animals or reptiles.

24 Therefore God gave them up in the lusts of their hearts to impurity, to the dishonoring of their bodies among themselves, 25 because they exchanged the truth about God for a lie and worshiped and served the creature rather than the Creator, who is blessed for ever! Amen.

26 For this reason God gave them up to dishonorable passions. Their women exchanged natural relations for unnatural, 27 and the men likewise gave up natural relations with women and were consumed with passion for one another, men committing shameless acts with men and receiving in their own persons the due penalty for their error.

28 And since they did not see fit to acknowledge God, God gave them up to a base mind and to improper conduct. 29 They were filled with all manner of wickedness, evil, covetousness, malice. Full of

envy, murder, strife, deceit, malignity, they are gossips, [30] slanderers, haters of God, insolent, haughty, boastful, inventors of evil, disobedient to parents, [31] foolish, faithless, heartless, ruthless. [32] Though they know God's decree that those who do such things deserve to die, they not only do them but approve those who practice them. ⌒

P aul's letter to the Romans stressed the new life available through faith. He announced that "the gospel . . . is the power of God for salvation to everyone who has faith" (Romans 1:16). Before taking up this theme, Paul dealt first with the question, "What is life like without God's salvation?"

When human beings disregard God and his commands, they sink into an ever worsening spiral of sinfulness. Paul wrote: "For although they knew God they did not honor him, . . . but they became futile in their thinking" (Romans 1:21). Apart from God, we cannot judge right from wrong. We easily confuse what is truly fulfilling with what is selfish and demeaning.

Paul catalogued the sins that entangle those who refuse "to acknowledge God" (Romans 1:28); they are "full of envy, murder, strife, deceit, malignity, they are gossips, slanderers, haters of God, insolent, haughty, boastful, inventors of evil, disobedient to parents, foolish, faithless, heartless, ruthless" (1:29-31). Men and women given over to a "debased mind" (1:28) abandon real love for the "degrading passions" of sexual impurity, including the practice of homosexuality, which Paul unequivocally condemned (1:27).

At the root of all their sins, such people have "exchanged the truth about God for a lie and worshiped and served the creature rather than the Creator" (Romans 1:25). Whenever we obey anyone or anything opposed to God, we sin. Herein lies the importance of the gospel: "In it the righteousness of God is revealed" (1:17). Many people today—even many Christians—prefer to ignore God's judgment against sin. We grow tolerant or numb toward sin because we lack confidence in God's ability to change us. But Paul also declared that the gospel "is the power of God for salvation to everyone who has faith" (1:16).

Paul did not deny human sinfulness; nor did he despair about it. He was convinced that in the gospel power is given for our victory over sin, for our salvation. This power gives strength to overcome the passions leading us to sin. It leads to wholeness and holiness. It is something God wants to give to us all, for God wants everyone to receive the fruit of righteousness through faith in Christ.

"Heavenly Father, you call me to participate in your divine life. I confess that I cannot save myself, yet I believe that in your Son is the power to live for you. May the power of the gospel strengthen me and change my life."

Romans 2:1-11

1   Therefore you have no excuse, O man, whoever you are, when you judge another; for in passing judgment upon him you condemn yourself, because you, the judge, are doing the very same things. 2 We know that the judgment of God rightly falls upon those who do such things. 3 Do you suppose, O man, that when you judge those who do such things and yet do them yourself, you will escape the judgment of God? 4 Or do you presume upon the riches of his kindness and forbearance

and patience? Do you not know that God's kindness is meant to lead you to repentance? [5] But by your hard and impenitent heart you are storing up wrath for yourself on the day of wrath when God's righteous judgment will be revealed. [6] For he will render to every man according to his works: [7] to those who by patience in well-doing seek for glory and honor and immortality, he will give eternal life; [8] but for those who are factious and do not obey the truth, but obey wickedness, there will be wrath and fury. [9] There will be tribulation and distress for every human being who does evil, the Jew first and also the Greek, [10] but glory and honor and peace for every one who does good, the Jew first and also the Greek. [11] For God shows no partiality. ✎

I n conformity to the Mosaic Law, the Jewish people during Jesus' time set themselves apart from Gentiles. They knew they were called to be holy by their God (Leviticus 19:2), so they set themselves apart from Gentiles and condemned them for their evil practices. Paul told the Jews that even through they were the chosen people, they had no right to condemn pagans. Why? Because the Jews were just as guilty of sin (in their own ways) as were the nonbelievers: "You, the judge, are doing the very same things" (Romans 2:1).

Paul focused on Christ and the life that comes from him. He stated his position clearly for both Jew and Gentile: "I am not ashamed of the gospel: it is the power of God for salvation to every one who has faith, to the Jew first and also to the Greek" (Romans 1:16). To Paul, only Jesus brought life and salvation; neither observance of law (the hope of the Pharisees) nor adherence to a philosophy or way of life (the practice of the Greeks) would bring true life.

Both Jews and Greeks will be judged not according to who they are, but by the lives they live based on faith in Jesus. Paul wrote: "To those who by patience in well-doing seek for glory and honor and immortality, he will give eternal life; but for those who are factious and do not obey the truth, but obey wickedness, there will be wrath and the fury" (Romans 2:7-8). We are called to have faith in Jesus and to live it.

All people, both Jew and Gentile, need to take Paul's words to heart. Do we believe that our salvation lies in Jesus Christ, and in him only? The world is not sympathetic with this view and in subtle—and not so subtle—ways we often follow the direction of the world. Let us pray that we will see the ways that we place our hope in our security, our identity, and our fulfillment rather than in Jesus.

"Heavenly Father, give me a pure heart which seeks only after Jesus. By your Spirit, help me to see those things in my life which I rely on for my security and salvation. Help me to see the treasure of the good news."

Romans 2:12-29

12 All who have sinned without the law will also perish without the law, and all who have sinned under the law will be judged by the law. 13 For it is not the hearers of the law who are righteous before God, but the doers of the law who will be justified. 14 When Gentiles who have not the law do by nature what the law requires, they are a law to themselves, even though they do not have the law. 15 They show that what the law requires is written on their hearts, while their conscience also bears witness and their conflicting thoughts accuse or perhaps excuse them 16 on that day when, according to my gospel, God judges the secrets of men by Christ Jesus.

[17] But if you call yourself a Jew and rely upon the law and boast of your relation to God [18] and know his will and approve what is excellent, because you are instructed in the law, [19] and if you are sure that you are a guide to the blind, a light to those who are in darkness, [20] a corrector of the foolish, a teacher of children, having in the law the embodiment of knowledge and truth— [21] you then who teach others, will you not teach yourself? While you preach against stealing, do you steal? [22] You who say that one must not commit adultery, do you commit adultery? You who abhor idols, do you rob temples? [23] You who boast in the law, do you dishonor God by breaking the law? [24] For, as it is written, "The name of God is blasphemed among the Gentiles because of you."

[25] Circumcision indeed is of value if you obey the law; but if you break the law, your circumcision becomes uncircumcision. [26] So, if a man who is uncircumcised keeps the precepts of the law, will not his uncircumcision be regarded as circumcision? [27] Then those who are physically uncircumcised but keep the law will condemn you who have the written code and circumcision but break the law. [28] For he is not a real Jew who is one outwardly, nor is true circumcision something external and physical. [29] He is a Jew who is one inwardly, and real circumcision is a matter of the heart, spiritual and not literal. His praise is not from men but from God.

I n Paul's day, many of the Jews prided themselves on being in a right relationship with God because of the covenant God made with them through Moses, a covenant he ratified through the law. Following this reasoning, they regarded Gentiles as morally lawless—not in a good relationship with God—since they did not share in a covenant relationship with God. Paul himself once thought that way, at least until his dramatic conversion and his experiences in the mission field taught him otherwise.

In a reversal of his earlier position, Paul reminded the Jewish Christians in Rome that what counts is not just hearing and knowing about the law but obeying it (Romans 2:13). He also pointed out that Gentiles, though without the law, can by nature do what is right and good if they follow the guidance of their conscience (2:15).

God alone knows the secrets of the human heart (Romans 2:16). In his mercy, he will judge all of us—Christians, Jews, Muslims, even unbelievers—according to how faithful we have been to what is in our heart and in light of our personal circumstances and heritage. As the Fathers of Vatican II explained in the *Dogmatic Constitution of the Church*:

> In view of the divine choice, they [Jews] are a people most dear for the sake of the fathers, for the gifts of God are without repentance (Romans 11:28-29). But the plan of salvation also includes those who acknowledge the Creator, in the first place amongst whom are the Muslims: these profess to hold the faith of Abraham, and together with us they adore the one, merciful God, mankind's judge on the last day.

> Nor is God remote from those who in shadows and images seek the unknown God, since he gives to all men life and

breath and all things (Acts 17:25-28), and since the Savior wills all men to be saved (1 Timothy 2:4). Those who, through no fault of their own, do not know the gospel of Christ or his church, but who nevertheless seek God with a sincere heart, and, moved by grace, try in their actions to do his will as they know it through the dictates of their conscience—those too may achieve eternal salvation.

Nor shall divine providence deny the assistance necessary for salvation to those who, without any fault of theirs, have not yet arrived at an explicit knowledge of God, and who, not without grace, strive to lead a good life. Whatever good or truth is found amongst them is considered by the church to be a preparation for the gospel and given by him who enlightens all men that they may at length have life. (*Lumen Gentium* II, 16)

"Thank you, Father, that in your great mercy you have opened the way to salvation for all of us!"

Romans 3:1-8

1   Then what advantage has the Jew? Or what is the value of circumcision? 2 Much in every way. To begin with, the Jews are entrusted with the oracles of God. 3 What if some were unfaithful? Does their faithlessness nullify the faithfulness of God? 4 By no means! Let God be true though every man be false, as it is written,
   "That thou mayest be justified in thy words,
   and prevail when thou art judged."

⁵ But if our wickedness serves to show the justice of God, what shall we say? That God is unjust to inflict wrath on us? (I speak in a human way.) ⁶ By no means! For then how could God judge the world? ⁷ But if through my falsehood God's truthfulness abounds to his glory, why am I still being condemned as a sinner? ⁸ And why not do evil that good may come?—as some people slanderously charge us with saying. Their condemnation is just. ✑

P aul argued that possessing "the oracles of God" is one of the Jews' chief advantages over the Gentiles (Romans 3:2). So what are these "oracles"? In simple terms, they are the word of God, his prophecies and promises. A fuller meaning, however, is that they are the way in which God reveals his plans and purposes, the way in which he communicated with his people. This is something greater than merely "possessing" the word of God in Scripture.

Paul reasoned that because they have been entrusted with these oracles, the Jewish people had a special relationship with God. They knew his will and were privileged with the calling to be guides to the blind and lights to those in darkness (Romans 2:19). They had special understanding that enabled them to teach children and correct those who had chosen folly (2:20).

These great privileges were both the Jews' advantage and the source of their unfaithfulness. They had such an exalted status, but many of them did not live a life worthy of the calling they had received. Still, Paul argued, their unfaithfulness did not push God to break the covenant. In one of the most dramatic statements of the New Testament, Paul wrote that God is true, even when everyone else is unfaithful (Romans 3:4).

This is the heart of the gospel. God will always remain faithful. He offers salvation to everyone, regardless of their sin and unfaithfulness. No one is excused, no one is overlooked by God, for all are under the same judgment, whether through the Jewish law or the dictates of the human conscience. God adheres firmly to all his promises. He does not lie, and he does not change his mind (Numbers 23:19).

In fact, God does not change at all! He declares it plainly himself: "I the LORD do not change" (Malachi 3:6). The apostle James echoes this statement, saying that with God the Father, "there is no variation or shadow due to change" (James 1:17). This truth is our anchor. Even in the midst of sin or guilt or failure, God is still with us. "I have loved you with an everlasting love; therefore I have continued my faithfulness to you" (Jeremiah 31:3). Brothers and sisters, we need to know the depth of God's love for us, so that we will stand firm, believing in his faithfulness.

"Father, you never change. Thank you for creating me out of love and loving me always. Touch my heart today with your love, that I might cling to you and uphold your faithfulness regardless of what this day brings."

Romans 3:9-20

9 What then? Are we Jews any better off? No, not at all; for I have already charged that all men, both Jews and Greeks, are under the power of sin, 10 as it is written:
 "None is righteous, no, not one;
 11 no one understands, no one seeks for God.
 12 All have turned aside, together they have gone wrong;
 no one does good, not even one."
 13 "Their throat is an open grave,
 they use their tongues to deceive."
 "The venom of asps is under their lips."
 14 "Their mouth is full of curses and bitterness."
 15 "Their feet are swift to shed blood,
 16 in their paths are ruin and misery,
 17 and the way of peace they do not know."
 18 "There is no fear of God before their eyes."
19 Now we know that whatever the law says it speaks to those who are under the law, so that every mouth may be stopped, and the whole world may be held accountable to God. 20 For no human being will be justified in his sight by works of the law, since through the law comes knowledge of sin. ✺

No human being will be justified in his sight by works of the law.
(Romans 3:20)

P aul continues his argument that Jews as well as Gentiles are outside of God's grace because of sin. Salvation through Christ is available "to every one who has faith, to the Jew first and also to the Greek" (Romans 1:16), precisely because it comes through faith and not through any other means. Not even Jews, who have the privilege of being God's chosen people, are exempted from divine judgment.

Up to this point, Paul has been presenting his case mainly on the basis of history and general observations about human behavior. But now he brings in a much stronger testimony than his own insights and interpretation of facts and events. To bring his argument home with full force, Paul turns to Scripture itself. Verses 10-18 of this passage are comprised of quotes from the Hebrew Scriptures—from the Psalms and Isaiah—that speak forcefully about the universal nature of sin. And then, to sum up his position, Paul writes, "We know that whatever the law says it speaks to those who are under the law, so that every mouth may be stopped" (Romans 3:19). Scripture has spoken; God himself has spoken. Who can possibly speak against him?

This shows how radically Paul trusts in the power of Scripture. It's not as if he thought the Bible was filled with spells and incantations that work magically to make a person think differently. Rather, he knew that Scripture is living and active, that it is not only God's word but also God's voice, which has the power to speak directly to the heart of anyone who listens humbly. Throughout this letter, we will see Paul piecing together quotes from Scripture, and not just to prove our sinfulness, but also to manifest the faithfulness, the love, and the incredible mercy of God the Father.

What's your experience of Scripture? Have there been times, whether at Mass or in prayer, when it seemed as if a line or a sentence jumped out at you and spoke directly to your situation? Have you known the power of Scripture to calm your fear, to give you wisdom for a situation, to convict you of a sin that needed confessing, or to fill you with joy? God *wants* to speak to us. He *wants* to form our minds and teach us. All he asks is that we spend time with his word, studying it, reflecting on it, and taking steps to put into practice what we believe we are hearing. He knows that as we do, we will become familiar with his voice, and our experience of his love and guidance will grow and deepen.

"Holy Spirit, teach me how to hear God's voice in Scripture. Open my ears as I open my heart. I want to know his still, small voice. I want to know his consolation, his wisdom, his love, and his guidance. But most of all, I want to know him as my Father."

Freedom from the Bondage of Sin

ROMANS
3:21–5:21

Romans 3:21-31

[21] But now the righteousness of God has been manifested apart from law, although the law and the prophets bear witness to it, [22] the righteousness of God through faith in Jesus Christ for all who believe. For there is no distinction; [23] since all have sinned and fall short of the glory of God, [24] they are justified by his grace as a gift, through the redemption which is in Christ Jesus, [25] whom God put forward as an expiation by his blood, to be received by faith. This was to show God's righteousness, because in his divine forbearance he had passed over former sins; [26] it was to prove at the present time that he himself is righteous and that he justifies him who has faith in Jesus.

[27] Then what becomes of our boasting? It is excluded. On what principle? On the principle of works? No, but on the principle of faith. [28] For we hold that a man is justified by faith apart from works of law. [29] Or is God the God of Jews only? Is he not the God of Gentiles also? Yes, of Gentiles also, [30] since God is one; and he will justify the circumcised on the ground of their faith and the uncircumcised through their faith. [31] Do we then overthrow the law by this faith? By no means! On the contrary, we uphold the law.

But now. . . (Romans 3:21)

Paul was a man devoted to the truth. As a Pharisee he had been trained to seek the truth and to act according to it. He knew the books of the Hebrew Bible and the teaching of the rabbis and did his best to live by it. He tried with all his heart and mind to be perfect before God.

When Paul was touched by the Lord, he came to see the truth even more clearly, recognizing the common condition of all people- that "all have sinned and fall short of the glory of God" (Romans 3:23; see also 1:21-25; 3:9-18). Our own experience confirms what is revealed in the Scriptures. All of us can recognize that there is an internal drive which compels us to do things which separate us from God and from one another. In this way we fall short or miss the mark of what God intends us to be. The Scriptures and our own experiences both demonstrate that no matter how hard we try, we can never measure up to God's standards on our own ability and strength.

Paul's introductory expression—"But now"—indicates that something tremendous has happened. Yes, we have sinned. Yes, we fall short of our goal. "But now" there is an answer which overcomes the past and the fallen human state, and that answer is Christ Jesus. The fact of Christ's coming into the world, taking on the burden of our sin, and paying the price for our sin, is greater than anything which happened in the past. In Christ Jesus, we are justified before God and this is a free gift available to everyone. It is received only by accepting Jesus and what he has done; it can never be earned by our own actions.

We need not be defeated by the gap between what we try so hard to do, and the failure we so often experience. Christ has delivered us from our condition of hopelessness and helplessness. All that is necessary is that we believe that Christ has done everything required to justify us before God. In truth, nothing we do can in any way add to the justification and righteousness that are ours in Christ.

Now, rather than trying to earn salvation, we can bear the fruit God desires by sharing with others the gift of new life which has been freely given us in Christ.

Romans 4:1-12

[1] What then shall we say about Abraham, our forefather according to the flesh? [2] For if Abraham was justified by works, he has something to boast about, but not before God. [3] For what does the scripture say? "Abraham believed God, and it was reckoned to him as righteousness." [4] Now to one who works, his wages are not reckoned as a gift but as his due. [5] And to one who does not work but trusts him who justifies the ungodly, his faith is reckoned as righteousness. [6] So also David pronounces a blessing upon the man to whom God reckons righteousness apart from works:

[7] "Blessed are those whose iniquities are forgiven,
and whose sins are covered;
[8] blessed is the man against whom the Lord will not reckon his sin."

[9] Is this blessing pronounced only upon the circumcised, or also upon the uncircumcised? We say that faith was reckoned to Abraham as righteousness. [10] How then was it reckoned to him? Was it before or after he had been circumcised? It was not after, but before he was circumcised. [11] He received circumcision as a sign or seal of the righteousness which he had by faith while he was still uncircumcised. The purpose was to make him the father of all who believe without being circumcised and who thus have righteousness reckoned to them, [12] and likewise the father of the circumcised who are not merely circumcised but also follow the example of the faith which our father Abraham had before he was circumcised.

As he explained the free gift of salvation in Christ, Paul pointed his readers back to an ancient hero of faith: Abraham, who "believed God, and it was reckoned to him as righteousness" (Romans 4:3; Genesis 15:6). Righteousness in this sense means being freed from sin and being set right in one's mind and heart. Abraham received this righteousness because he trusted in God's promise to him and strove to act according to that trust. Seeing such faith, God drew Abraham close to his heart and called him his friend. When we believe in Jesus and embrace his salvation, God declares us righteous as well. He calls us his friend!

A righteous person acts according to God's will. But here is where we can get confused. We do not become righteous because of our actions. Our righteous acts flow from the change brought about in us when we embraced Jesus. The good we do now reflects the goodness that God has brought about in us.

If we continue to seek Jesus and the Father, we will see more clearly both our need for God and the limitless love that he has for us. We will stop trying hard to earn his love and will instead come to rest in him, secure in the knowledge that he has won the victory over our sin. When the Holy Spirit helps us to recognize our sin or our weakness, we can turn to God in repentance and receive the forgiveness that he has already made available through the death of his Son. Such a blessing will bring us in touch with the Father's loving heart and melt our resistance to his call to love and forgive those around us.

Jesus taught that "If you would believe, you would see the glory of God" (John 11:40). Abraham believed, and he saw God's promise come true in the birth of his son Isaac. Our own belief in God will bring us to the realization of God's promise of peace in this life and union with him in eternity. Let us make him the cornerstone of our lives!

"Jesus, thank you for the gift of your righteousness. You offer us the same freedom and closeness with you that you offered Abraham. Help me to believe in you in all circumstances, as Abraham did, and to keep my heart fixed on your great love."

Romans 4:13-17

[13] The promise to Abraham and his descendants, that they should inherit the world, did not come through the law but through the righteousness of faith. [14] If it is the adherents of the law who are to be the heirs, faith is null and the promise is void. [15] For the law brings wrath, but where there is no law there is no transgression. [16] That is why it depends on faith, in order that the promise may rest on grace and be guaranteed to all his descendants—not only to the adherents of the law but also to those who share the faith of Abraham, for he is the father of us all, [17] as it is written, "I have made you the father of many nations"—in the presence of the God in whom he believed, who gives life to the dead and calls into existence the things that do not exist. ⤙

Some Jewish converts to the Christian way of life believed that God chose Abraham to be the father of his people because he was the only righteous man of his time, a unique person. Having refuted the arguments of these Jewish Christians concerning justification by circumcision and works of the law (Romans 4:1-12), Paul addressed their delusion that salvation was based on physical descent from Abraham and observance of the law. He pointed to God's promise to Abraham and declared that justification for both Jew and Gentile is based on faith (4:13-18).

The promise, "I will make of you a great nation . . . and by you all the families of the earth shall bless themselves" (Genesis 12:2-3), was totally unmerited. It had nothing to do with the race, status, or faithfulness of the first receiver of the promise. It was a promise emerging solely from the generosity of God and requiring only that one be found in the same disposition of faith as Abraham himself.

Justification in God's sight is not our own doing; "it is the gift of God" (Ephesians 2:8). It is not a reward for faithful observance of the law. Of itself the Mosaic Law was both good and holy because it revealed God's will, but it provided no spiritual power for obeying it. Law makes us aware of sin but has a capacity to draw us into longing for what is unlawful. As we descend from unlawful desire to sinful acts of rebellion against God, we tend to expect judgment, rather than justification, at God's hands.

God has made known a new and glorious way for all peoples alike to enter into a right relationship with him through faith in his Son, Jesus. For all of us, the message of Paul is the same. Righteousness before God does not depend upon the circumstances of our birth, our acts of worship, or good works, or our attempts at self-discipline. It is ours when we are united with Christ through baptism and faith, live in the power of the Spirit of Christ, and do the works made known to us by the Spirit. Our hope must be in God only for he is always faithful to his promises.

"Loving Father, help me to believe in Jesus and to trust in him only for my life and eternal salvation. Help me to know him, so that I might trust him."

Romans 4:18-25

[18] In hope he believed against hope, that he should become the father of many nations; as he had been told, "So shall your descendants be." [19] He did not weaken in faith when he considered his own body, which was as good as dead because he was about a hundred years old, or when he considered the barrenness of Sarah's womb. [20] No distrust made him waver concerning the promise of God, but he grew strong in his faith as he gave glory to God, [21] fully convinced that God was able to do what he had promised. [22] That is why his faith was "reckoned to him as righteousness." [23] But the words, "it was reckoned to him," were written not for his sake alone, [24] but for ours also. It will be reckoned to us who believe in him that raised from the dead Jesus our Lord, [25] who was put to death for our trespasses and raised for our justification. ✍

Paul continues with the account of Abraham to show that we are justified by our faith in God, not by our adherence to the law. Abraham had no practical reason to believe that he and Sarah could have a child in their old age. Yet hope for an heir consumed his heart! God had promised that a son would be born to him and that Abraham would be the "father of a multitude of nations" (Genesis 17:5; Romans 4:17). Abraham believed that his Creator, the one who called him into being, would be faithful to the promise he had made. He gave glory to his maker by acknowledging his total confidence in him.

This abiding trust found favor with God. Abraham was "fully convinced that God was able to do what he had promised. That is why his faith was 'reckoned to him as righteousness'" in the sight of God (Romans 4:21-22). As the years passed without any sign of the awaited child, Abraham's faith was tested. His perseverance transformed him into a man who truly pleased God, a man whose hope remained in God alone. He did not waver through unbelief (4:20).

God was under no obligation to Abraham because of any good works on Abraham's part. Instead, God credited righteousness to Abraham because he relied on the strength and faithfulness of the one who had promised. This faith of Abraham's was not mere passive resignation. Rather, it was bold and courageous as he dared to set his heart on that which seemed impossible. His confidence was in the identity of the one who had promised.

Paul used this example of Abraham to challenge the Romans (and us) to see if we are fully convinced that God has the power and the desire to provide what he has promised. This is the lesson we can learn from Abraham's life: God will credit us as righteous if we walk in faith in God. When we remain confident of God's faithfulness we are pleasing to God. We don't have to rely on our own efforts or works to make us right with God, for God provides the way for us through Jesus. As for our works, they flow out of this faith.

"Lord, our faith and our hope are in you. We have come to believe that Jesus Christ is the complete fulfillment of all your promises."

Romans 5:1-5

[1] Therefore, since we are justified by faith, we have peace with God through our Lord Jesus Christ. [2] Through him we have obtained access to this grace in which we stand, and we rejoice in our hope of sharing the glory of God. [3] More than that, we rejoice in our sufferings, knowing that suffering produces endurance, [4] and endurance produces character, and character produces hope, [5] and hope does not disappoint us, because God's love has been poured into our hearts through the Holy Spirit which has been given to us.

God's love has been poured into our hearts through the Holy Spirit.
(Romans 5:5)

Paul knew with an absolute certainty that God loved him. He could write so vividly to the Romans about God's love because he had experienced it in a profound way. He also knew just as certainly that through Jesus' death, he had been reconciled to God and was at peace with him. Freed from sin and guilt, he knew that he could place his hope and confidence in the promise of sharing in God's glory in heaven (Romans 5:1-2).

Paul's sure knowledge that he had been reconciled to God and his personal experience of God's love were the foundation stones on which he built his entire Christian life. Filled with this love which the Spirit had poured like cool, refreshing water into his heart (Romans 5:5), he was able to face difficulties—both everyday struggles and major challenges—joyfully.

Moreover, Paul realized that it was through such difficulties that God was strengthening and bringing him to maturity. Consequently, as Paul encountered the demands and hardships of living in this world and preaching the gospel, he could meet them with patience and hope (5:3-4). He knew that sin, evil, and suffering would never get the final word. Instead, firmly grounded in the love of his Father in heaven, he almost looked forward to what God could accomplish in him through them.

We can know the love of God with the same certainty that Paul did for we, too, have been reconciled to God. We too have the exact same access to God's grace that Paul had (Romans 5:1-2). Every day, God invites us to take our stand in him. He longs to see us place our trust in his passionate, personal love for us. The more we open ourselves to God's love in this way, the more we will be equipped to face the challenges of life with peace, patience, and even hope.

As you go through your day, look for ways you can yield to the work of the Holy Spirit in you. Let God have his way in renewing your mind and forming your character. This is the promise of the gospel: The more we are immersed in God's love, the deeper and stronger our hope will be. And this hope will never be disappointed.

"Holy Spirit, pour more of God's love into my heart. I want to yield to your work in me today as I live in the hope of sharing the glory of God."

Romans 5:6-11

6   While we were still weak, at the right time Christ died for the ungodly. 7 Why, one will hardly die for a righteous man—though perhaps for a good man one will dare even to die. 8 But God shows his love for us in that while we were yet sinners Christ died for us. 9 Since, therefore, we are now justified by his blood, much more shall we be saved by him from the wrath of God. 10 For if while we were enemies we were reconciled to God by the death of his Son, much more, now that we are reconciled, shall we be saved by his life. 11 Not only so, but we also rejoice in God through our Lord Jesus Christ, through whom we have now received our reconciliation.

Maximilian Kolbe was a Conventual Franciscan priest from Poland in the middle of the twentieth century. Rounded up during the Nazi invasion of Poland, Kolbe was sent to Auschwitz. When Francis Gajowniczek, a fellow Polish soldier, was sentenced to be starved to death in retaliation for an escaped prisoner, Kolbe offered his life in place of the condemned man. "I am a Catholic priest from Poland," he announced to the startled German commandant. "I would like to take his place, because he has a wife and children." Thus Kolbe, condemned to die instead of Gajowniczek, became a martyr of love.

It is an extraordinary kind of love that enables a person to die willingly for another as Maximilian Kolbe did. As Paul pointed out to the Romans, it is rare for a man to be prepared to give up his own life for someone else, even if that someone else is a very good person (Romans 5:7). Yet how much greater is God's love for us, far surpassing that of any human being! "While we were yet sinners Christ died for us" (5:8). "While we were enemies, we were reconciled to God by the death of his Son" (5:10).

Through Jesus' death, the whole human race—weak and ungodly as we are—has been pardoned. Peace has been established between God and his creation. That is what Paul means when he says that we are "justified by [Christ's] blood" (Romans 5:9). As St. Augustine once put it, "Christ loved us in our unloveliness, in order to make us beautiful like himself."

Yes, we have already been justified and reconciled to God, but we are still in the process of being "saved by his life" (5:10). Day by day, God wants to penetrate our hearts and minds more deeply and bring about his full salvation in every area of our lives. He wants to take all of our unruly emotions and sinful thoughts and transform them, making us "beautiful like himself." As we cooperate with the Holy Spirit working in us, we will come, at the end of each day, to look at bit more like Jesus than the previous day.

"Father, I am overwhelmed by your great love for me! Thank you for reconciling me to yourself through the blood of your Son Jesus. May I grow to reflect his likeness more each day."

Romans 5:12-21

[12] Therefore as sin came into the world through one man and death through sin, and so death spread to all men because all men sinned— [13] sin indeed was in the world before the law was given, but sin is not counted where there is no law. [14] Yet death reigned from Adam to Moses, even over those whose sins were not like the transgression of Adam, who was a type of the one who was to come.

¹⁵ But the free gift is not like the trespass. For if many died through one man's trespass, much more have the grace of God and the free gift in the grace of that one man Jesus Christ abounded for many. ¹⁶ And the free gift is not like the effect of that one man's sin. For the judgment following one trespass brought condemnation, but the free gift following many trespasses brings justification. ¹⁷ If, because of one man's trespass, death reigned through that one man, much more will those who receive the abundance of grace and the free gift of righteousness reign in life through the one man Jesus Christ.

¹⁸ Then as one man's trespass led to condemnation for all men, so one man's act of righteousness leads to acquittal and life for all men. ¹⁹ For as by one man's disobedience many were made sinners, so by one man's obedience many will be made righteous. ²⁰ Law came in, to increase the trespass; but where sin increased, grace abounded all the more, ²¹ so that, as sin reigned in death, grace also might reign through righteousness to eternal life through Jesus Christ our Lord.

The sin of our first parents has had a profound effect. Through their disobedience, sin was unleashed on the whole world. From that day onward, sin has rampaged with its power to alienate us from our heavenly Father and from one another. Even before there was a law to disobey, sin's primary effects—separation from God, mistrust, selfishness, even death—have oppressed humankind (Romans 5:14). That is how vast and how far-reaching are the effects of original sin.

If we look at the world in that light, the outlook seems pretty bleak. Thankfully, we don't live only in that light. We are no longer under the reign of sin. We are under grace—God's overflowing, abundant mercy and provision. Through Jesus' sacrifice on the cross, our Father has ransomed us from death. He broke sin's iron grip and forgave each of us individually when we were baptized. Every day, he offers us the grace to remain faithful to him until we can see him face to face in heaven.

But there is more to our lives than the future hope of heaven. All throughout our lives, God is raining down grace so lavishly that we can actually be transformed into his image right now! We don't have to focus solely on avoiding sin. We can become living witnesses to the righteousness and power of Jesus Christ. Only the grace of God—as we cooperate with him—can change our hearts, renew our minds, and teach us to live in love.

We aren't perfect. We don't always act righteously. We can't change by our own efforts alone. But we do have this assurance: Where sin abounds, grace abounds all the more (Romans 5:20). God's free gift of grace is extravagant and inexhaustible. Today, put aside human striving and resolve to receive grace. Our Father is pouring a mighty flood of his love, mercy, and favor for all who will turn to him and receive it. May grace "reign through righteousness" in all our lives (5:21)!

"Father, I praise you for your grace. In love, you soften my heart and tame my thoughts. Thank you for Jesus' death, but also for his life. Because of him, I can be carried on the tide of grace to your heavenly throne."

From Death to Life

ROMANS
6:1–7:25

Romans 6:1-11

[1] What shall we say then? Are we to continue in sin that grace may abound? [2] By no means! How can we who died to sin still live in it? [3] Do you not know that all of us who have been baptized into Christ Jesus were baptized into his death? [4] We were buried therefore with him by baptism into death, so that as Christ was raised from the dead by the glory of the Father, we too might walk in newness of life. [5] For if we have been united with him in a death like his, we shall certainly be united with him in a resurrection like his. [6] We know that our old self was crucified with him so that the sinful body might be destroyed, and we might no longer be enslaved to sin. [7] For he who has died is freed from sin. [8] But if we have died with Christ, we believe that we shall also live with him. [9] For we know that Christ being raised from the dead will never die again; death no longer has dominion over him. [10] The death he died he died to sin, once for all, but the life he lives he lives to God. [11] So you also must consider yourselves dead to sin and alive to God in Christ Jesus.

St. Paul declared to the Romans one of the central truths of our faith: When Jesus died on the cross he put to death our old fallen nature with all its sinful passions and drives. Triumphing over sin, he rose from the grave to a new and glorious life—and he took us with him!

The simple, yet incredible, truth is that when we are baptized into Christ, our sinful nature actually dies with him (Romans 6:6). Crucified with Christ, we are freed from sin and come to share in the new and glorious nature of the risen Jesus (6:11). In this transformation is our hope for eternal life. It is what makes us children of God.

Through baptism, we were committed to putting sin to death within ourselves, and now in practice we are called to do so. God wants each of us to take that basic "yes" to him which was part of our baptism and repeat it every day, in every situation we face. The degree to which we allow the truth of our death and resurrection with Christ to take hold of our day-to-day lives is the degree to which we will know freedom from sin and deeper intimacy with Jesus.

We all know that none of us will be completely purified of sin when we die. Yes, we have died and risen with Christ. Yes, we are sons and daughters of God. And yet there will remain areas in our lives which we have not yet fully surrendered to the Lord. But if heaven is a place of complete holiness, how will we ever make it in?

This is how the doctrine of purgatory developed within the church. Purgatory is understood to be the state or "place" in which everyone who has died in Christ is purified of the last remaining vestiges of sin. While we might consider purgatory to be a place of final suffering, a more accurate description would probably be a place of great hope and eager expectation. Who among us, having fought the good fight during our lives, would not long to be completely purified? We are not being punished, but conformed to Christ. We are not suffering, but cooperating with Jesus as he brings to completion the great work he began at our baptism.

Let us rejoice today in the completeness of the salvation Jesus has won for us. Let us ask the Holy Spirit to continue his great work of purification in us today. Great is our heritage, and secure is our hope!

"God, our Creator and Redeemer, by your power Jesus conquered sin and death. May all your people who have gone before us in faith share in his victory and enjoy the vision of your glory forever."

Romans 6:12-18

^{12} Let not sin therefore reign in your mortal bodies, to make you obey their passions. ^{13} Do not yield your members to sin as instruments of wickedness, but yield yourselves to God as men who have been brought from death to life, and your members to God as instruments of righteousness. ^{14} For sin will have no dominion over you, since you are not under law but under grace.

^{15} What then? Are we to sin because we are not under law but under grace? By no means! ^{16} Do you not know that if you yield yourselves to any one as obedient slaves, you are slaves of the one whom you obey, either of sin, which leads to death, or of obedience, which leads to righteousness? ^{17} But thanks be to God, that you who were once slaves of sin have become obedient from the heart to the standard of teaching to which you were committed, ^{18} and, having been set free from sin, have become slaves of righteousness.

In Christ Jesus, Christians are free of the power of sin. Paul wrote: "Sin will have no dominion over you, since you are not under law but under grace" (Romans 6:14). If this is the promise made to us, why do we so often fall to sin? Why does sin have such power over us? To understand this, we must know who we are as people infected by sin.

Our first parents, created in God's image and likeness, chose to disobey him. The result was separation and alienation from God for themselves and for all people. But in his mercy, God did not abandon us. Rather, the grace of God appeared for the salvation of all (Titus 2:11). We are made righteous only by faith in Jesus and what he did by his death and resurrection (Romans 3:22). Salvation is a gift (3:24), freely given by our God through faith in Christ.

In faith and baptism, we are united with Christ and his victory over sin. We experience freedom over the power of sin when we make a decision to live no longer the Adam life but to let Christ live in us through his Spirit. Grace, which is the power of the Holy Spirit in us, renders sin and Satan powerless. As our hearts are transformed, we take on the heart of Christ. This enables us to love God, to trust him, and to obey his commands.

As we embrace Christ and his life more fully, we experience true inner spiritual change. A new spirit comes to maturity in us, a spirit open to grace. Our separation and alienation from God will diminish as we allow Jesus to dwell in us in accord with our baptism into him. He died to save us, and we love him and embrace him. Our old nature is transformed as we learn that in Christ and through him all things are possible. More and more, we experience the truth that sin has no power over us as we live the life of grace.

Let us ask the Spirit to help us receive more fully the grace of the new life in Christ. Let us also allow the Lord to reign in us so that we would more and more know the victory over sin that is ours in Christ Jesus.

Romans 6:19-23

¹⁹ I am speaking in human terms, because of your natural limitations. For just as you once yielded your members to impurity and to greater and greater iniquity, so now yield your members to righteousness for sanctification.
²⁰ When you were slaves of sin, you were free in regard to righteousness. ²¹ But then what return did you get from the things of which you are now ashamed? The end of those things is death.
²² But now that you have been set free from sin and have become slaves of God, the return you get is sanctification and its end, eternal life. ²³ For the wages of sin is death, but the free gift of God is eternal life in Christ Jesus our Lord. ✍

Just as you once yielded your members to . . . iniquity, so now yield your members to righteousness for sanctification. (Romans 6:19)

We were once slaves to sin (Romans 6:20), obeying it as our master. Now, through the grace and love of our Lord Jesus Christ, we are able to obey God, to present ourselves as slaves to righteousness. Paul said that Christians are freed from sin and enslaved to God (6:22), but what kind of freedom is that?

We usually understand freedom to mean being liberated from restraint in choosing and pursuing our own ideas. Paul held that it is impossible for a person to live in total independence, being subject to no one. He argued that the freedom from sin achieved by Jesus' death and resurrection did not mean total and complete human independence, but rather acceptance of another master, acceptance of God. This new life in Christ is not slavery, as it is known among people; it is the highest and only freedom.

How do we find this freedom? As we learn to trust in the leadings of the Holy Spirit, we begin to change, to be healed, to be submitted to Christ. As we embrace Christ, we are cleansed of our sins, our guilt disappears, our fallen patterns are put to death, and we are made alive (Romans 6:4).

How can we present ourselves as slaves to righteousness? We start by allowing the Holy Spirit to change our way of thinking; in essence, we put on the mind of Christ. Instead of thinking about ourselves and our concerns all day, we commence each day with prayer, committing our lives to Jesus and seeking God's wisdom. If we do not daily seek God's revelation in prayer, we may revert to our old ways of looking for fulfillment in old patterns of sin. As we put on the mind of Christ, we can fix our thoughts on God and how much he loves us. We will be drawn into that same powerful love that drew Jesus to perfect obedience.

More and more, we will be able to love and forgive our families, to reach out to those who are suffering, to pray for a world in turmoil. This happens in all those who present themselves as slaves to righteousness consecrated to the master of righteousness.

Romans 7:1-12

1   Do you not know, brethren—for I am speaking to those who know the law—that the law is binding on a person only during his life? 2 Thus a married woman is bound by law to her husband as long as he lives; but if her husband dies she is discharged from the law concerning the husband. 3 Accordingly, she will be called an

adulteress if she lives with another man while her husband is alive. But if her husband dies she is free from that law, and if she marries another man she is not an adulteress.

4   Likewise, my brethren, you have died to the law through the body of Christ, so that you may belong to another, to him who has been raised from the dead in order that we may bear fruit for God. 5 While we were living in the flesh, our sinful passions, aroused by the law, were at work in our members to bear fruit for death. 6 But now we are discharged from the law, dead to that which held us captive, so that we serve not under the old written code but in the new life of the Spirit.

7   What then shall we say? That the law is sin? By no means! Yet, if it had not been for the law, I should not have known sin. I should not have known what it is to covet if the law had not said, "You shall not covet." 8 But sin, finding opportunity in the commandment, wrought in me all kinds of covetousness. Apart from the law sin lies dead. 9 I was once alive apart from the law, but when the commandment came, sin revived and I died; 10 the very commandment which promised life proved to be death to me. 11 For sin, finding opportunity in the commandment, deceived me and by it killed me. 12 So the law is holy, and the commandment is holy and just and good. 🖋

The law is holy, and the commandment is holy and just and good.
(Romans 7:12)

Here's a puzzle worth unraveling. The law God gave to Moses was meant to restrain our all-too-human tendency toward evil—yet sin undeniably abounds to this day. In fact, the law seems to provoke the very tendencies it's supposed to control. Why would this be? Paul explains that it's because sin finds "opportunity in the commandment" (Romans 7:8). In other words, sin is so deceptive it can even take what is good and twist it to its own ends.

Well then, if the law is good, and if God's commandments are holy, why aren't they the remedy for sin? Because God has a better way, a way in which sin can find no opportunity. We call that way *grace*, and it is the only true weapon against sin. We all know that grace: Jesus' death on the cross for us, destroying the sin we could never overcome on our own. Because we have died with Christ, we have entered into a new relationship with the law (Romans 7:1-3). It remains a guide, but *Jesus himself* has now become our keeper. His grace and power, active within us, can keep us pure and holy.

This was Paul's breakthrough discovery: We are bound to grace as fully as a wife is bound to her husband! Does that mean we can ignore the law? No, it means that instead of relying on the law, we are meant to rely on Jesus, who has perfectly fulfilled the law (Matthew 5:17) in a way that we, by our own efforts, could never accomplish. Human effort—as necessary as it is—simply cannot produce a life pleasing to God. All our efforts must be coupled with and undergirded by grace.

Every day, God showers us with grace: with patience to deal with whining children; peace as a loved one suffers; kindness to a neighbor who has offended us; wisdom in a perplexing situation; self-control in the face of temptation. Sometimes God simply allows us to know his love and presence in our lives. All this is grace, meant to keep us from sin and enable us to serve God and others. We cannot get along without it!

"Glory to you, Father! You soak me with your grace, regardless of my worthiness. You are all-loving, gentle and kind with me, strengthening and supporting me by your grace. I want to praise you today in my words and actions."

Romans 7:13-25

[13] Did that which is good, then, bring death to me? By no means! It was sin, working death in me through what is good, in order that sin might be shown to be sin, and through the commandment might become sinful beyond measure. [14] We know that the law is spiritual; but I am carnal, sold under sin. [15] I do not understand my own actions. For I do not do what I want, but I do the very thing I hate. [16] Now if I do what I do not want, I agree that the law is good. [17] So then it is no longer I that do it, but sin which dwells within me. [18] For I know that nothing good dwells within me, that is, in my flesh. I can will what is right, but I cannot do it. [19] For I do not do the good I want, but the evil I do not want is what I do. [20] Now if I do what I do not want, it is no longer I that do it, but sin which dwells within me.

[21] So I find it to be a law that when I want to do right, evil lies close at hand. [22] For I delight in the law of God, in my inmost self, [23] but I see in my members another law at war with the law of my mind and making me captive to the law of sin which dwells in my members. [24] Wretched man that I am! Who will deliver me from this body of death? [25] Thanks be to God through Jesus Christ our Lord! So then, I of myself serve the law of God with my mind, but with my flesh I serve the law of sin. ✍

All Christians should start each day believing that with God's help things will be different and they will be able to live for the Lord and not give in to temptations, angers, or fears. We often start the day with the best of intentions, but as it wears on we experience a sense of discouragement as we fall into sin patterns and act as if we do not know the Lord. St. Paul understood this frustration we experience when the desire to do what is right is overcome by the power of sin (Romans 7:19-20).

Paul knew that the sin within him had authority over his fallen human nature. He further understood that there were two forces contending for control of him. One was the inner desire of his spirit to be like Christ. The other was his fallen nature which sought self-gain and pleasure. Paul asked: "Wretched man that I am! Who will deliver me from this body of death?" He answered his own question: "Thanks be to God through Jesus Christ our Lord!" (Romans 7:24-25).

Paul had come to realize what every Christian must learn: The thrust of our fallen natures can never be altered to be pleasing to God, but must die. We should not be surprised to discover sinful drives within us. At the same time, however, God has rescued us from sin by enabling us to be united with Christ in his death and also in his resurrection. The Spirit of Jesus in us by faith and baptism gives us power to live godly lives not found in our unredeemed natures.

How can we appropriate Jesus' victory over sin? God longs to pour out grace, and does so through prayer, the sacraments, and Scripture reading. Too often, however, we allow the press of daily responsibilities, the pursuit of worldly pleasure, or other distractions to keep us so occupied that we do not open ourselves to God's grace. Receiving the power to live victorious Christian lives is a daily activity that requires us to turn to God and grow with him.

"Father, give us the strength to overcome our preoccupations so that we can resist the distractions of the world and turn to you for the grace you long to give us. Empower us through the Holy Spirit to live for Christ."

Living by the Spirit

ROMANS
8:1-39

Romans 8:1-11

1   There is therefore now no condemnation for those who are in Christ Jesus. 2 For the law of the Spirit of life in Christ Jesus has set me free from the law of sin and death. 3 For God has done what the law, weakened by the flesh, could not do: sending his own Son in the likeness of sinful flesh and for sin, he condemned sin in the flesh, 4 in order that the just requirement of the law might be fulfilled in us, who walk not according to the flesh but according to the Spirit. 5 For those who live according to the flesh set their minds on the things of the flesh, but those who live according to the Spirit set their minds on the things of the Spirit. 6 To set the mind on the flesh is death, but to set the mind on the Spirit is life and peace. 7 For the mind that is set on the flesh is hostile to God; it does not submit to God's law, indeed it cannot; 8 and those who are in the flesh cannot please God. 9   But you are not in the flesh, you are in the Spirit, if in fact the Spirit of God dwells in you. Any one who does not have the Spirit of Christ does not belong to him. 10 But if Christ is in you, although your bodies are dead because of sin, your spirits are alive because of righteousness. 11 If the Spirit of him who raised Jesus from the dead dwells in you, he who raised Christ Jesus from the dead will give life to your mortal bodies also through his Spirit which dwells in you. ✺

The Mosaic Law was given to the Israelites to teach them how God wanted them to live. Try as they might, however, they could never live up to the law because the power of sin in them was stronger than their desire to obey God. But God did what the law, weakened by our flesh, could not do. He sent his own Son—a man just like us—to deal with sin, so that we might now walk according to the Spirit (Romans 8:3-4).

All Christians should start their day with a fundamental decision that they are going to live by the power of the Holy Spirit, not by the power of their own flesh. "Flesh" (as used by Paul in this context) refers to human nature unaided by the Holy Spirit. Apart from God, human nature since the fall has been, is, and always will be opposed to God. Jesus' victory over sin becomes our victory and will have an effect on our lives as we embrace the truth that we can avoid the flesh only by seeking out the life of God's Holy Spirit each day.

A question that often comes to mind is: "How can I tell if I am living by the power of the Holy Spirit at a given moment of the day, or if I am living by the flesh?" St. Paul answered: "To set the mind on the flesh is death, but to set the mind on the Spirit is life and peace" (Romans 8:6). We can examine ourselves periodically during the day to see if we are experiencing peace, joy, love, and the other fruit of the Spirit (Galatians 5:22-23).

If we are not, but rather see anger, frustration, or division, we have probably slipped back into living according to the flesh (Galatians 5:19-21). When we see this, we should not fall into self-condemnation, for "there is no condemnation for those who are in Christ Jesus" (Romans 8:1). Instead, we can repent and recommit ourselves to live by the Spirit. And we can strengthen ourselves through the Eucharist, prayer, and the word of God. This is what the saints of the church have always done.

"Lord Jesus, I want to live by your Spirit today and each day. Help me to discern when I am in the Spirit and when I am in the flesh. Give me the grace to repent quickly when I find that I have strayed. I want your victory over sin to be mine today."

Romans 8:12-17

[12] So then, brethren, we are debtors, not to the flesh, to live according to the flesh— [13] for if you live according to the flesh you will die, but if by the Spirit you put to death the deeds of the body you will live. [14] For all who are led by the Spirit of God are sons of God. [15] For you did not receive the spirit of slavery to fall back into fear, but you have received the spirit of sonship. When we cry, "Abba! Father!" [16] it is the Spirit himself bearing witness with our spirit that we are children of God, [17] and if children, then heirs, heirs of God and fellow heirs with Christ, provided we suffer with him in order that we may also be glorified with him. ☙

We all have daily duties and obligations: to produce at work, to pay our bills, to care for our families. In the same way, we have an obligation to God to put off the fallen nature and live a new life in Christ (Romans 8:12-13). This duty is more important than any of our other duties because it affects our eternal life. By our own efforts, however, it is impossible to carry out this duty. It is God's work in us. Only the Holy Spirit can give us the power to live new lives. "By the Spirit you put to death the deeds of the body" (8:13). "All who are led by the Spirit of God are sons of God" (8:14).

We must be confident that the Holy Spirit dwells in us and will lead us. "Do you not know that you are God's temple and God's Spirit dwells in you?" (1 Corinthians 3:16). The Scriptures are full of ways in which the Holy Spirit leads us. He will guide us into all truth and explain the word of God to us (John 16:13). He will help us to overcome our areas of weakness (Romans 8:26). He will convict us of our sins and lead us to repentance (John 16:8). As we try to serve the Lord, the Holy Spirit will direct us in all we say to him (Matthew 10:20). He will lead us in the way of sanctification, guaranteeing our place in heaven with the Father (Ephesians 1:13-14).

To experience the glory and the joy of new life in Christ, we must be attentive to the working of the Holy Spirit within us. If we are not obedient, we will be powerless. Through obedience, however, we can receive blessings, clarity and power. As the Spirit reveals the meaning of Scripture to us, we must take it upon ourselves to conform ourselves to God's word. The more obedient we are to the promptings of God through the Holy Spirit, the fuller will be our experience of God and his presence in our lives. Obedience assures fulfillment.

"Spirit of the living God, help us to know your presence within us. Guide us in every step of our Christian lives; help us to be attentive to the work of the Father in our lives and to respond obediently to his commands."

Romans 8:18-25

18 I consider that the sufferings of this present time are not worth comparing with the glory that is to be revealed to us. 19 For the creation waits with eager longing for the revealing of the sons of God; 20 for the creation was subjected to futility, not of its own will but by the will of him who subjected it in hope; 21 because the creation itself will be set free from its bondage to decay and obtain

the glorious liberty of the children of God. [22] We know that the whole creation has been groaning in travail together until now; [23] and not only the creation, but we ourselves, who have the first fruits of the Spirit, groan inwardly as we wait for adoption as sons, the redemption of our bodies. [24] For in this hope we were saved. Now hope that is seen is not hope. For who hopes for what he sees? [25] But if we hope for what we do not see, we wait for it with patience.

While Paul well knew the difficulty of living for God in this world, he also knew the glorious destiny that lies ahead for all who live in Christ (Romans 8:18). Those who live by faith and rely on the Spirit dwelling in them taste even now the first fruits of the full harvest to come (8:23). Through baptism, we have become sons and daughters of God and receive a share of his life. Living in hope, we wait in joyful expectation for the coming of Christ and full participation in our promised inheritance.

Paul saw all of creation groaning and in travail. Even though we have the first fruits of the Spirit, we groan as we await our full adoption and the redemption of our bodies (Romans 8:23). For Paul, the pain and sufferings of this life were real, but they could not compare to the coming glory. He saw our groaning to be like a woman in childbirth. She experiences pain—but with the expectancy of life. Her pain is couched in hope, and she has confidence that her suffering will at last bring about that for which she has waited for such a long time.

Fr. Raniero Cantalamessa, O.F.M. Cap., papal preacher and retreat director, in his book *Life in the Lordship of Jesus*, puts it this way:

> The state of believers in the world . . . is a state taut between the 'already' and the 'not yet'. . . . The prayer of a redeemed man springs exactly from the tension between faith and hope, between what we already possess and what we still hope for. Fundamentally, it is an agonizing yearning for the full freedom of the children of God and for glory.

Paul would not have denied that the world can be a place of great sorrow. However, instead of focusing on this, he directed our gaze forward in hope to what is to come. The Holy Spirit, the first fruit of our redemption, our down payment on eternal life, is our ground for this great hope. Satan, however, continues to do all that he can to thwart God's work in us and will continue to do so until the end. His only desire is to keep us from yielding to the work of God and persevering in his will.

In hope, we are to wait with patient endurance (Romans 8:25). Living life in the Spirit, receiving the Eucharist, being prayerful, reading Scripture, repenting and remaining close to Jesus—all these will strengthen, sustain, and purify us as we wait for the full harvest.

Romans 8:26-30

[26] Likewise the Spirit helps us in our weakness; for we do not know how to pray as we ought, but the Spirit himself intercedes for us with sighs too deep for words. [27] And he who searches the hearts of men knows what is the mind of the Spirit, because the Spirit intercedes for the saints according to the will of God.
[28] We know that in everything God works for good with those who love him, who are called according to his purpose. [29] For those whom he foreknew he also predestined to be conformed to the image of his Son, in order that he might be the first-born among many brethren. [30] And those whom he predestined he also called; and those whom he called he also justified; and those whom he justified he also glorified.

How encouraging it is to know that the Holy Spirit is always interceding for us (Romans 8:26-27). The Spirit takes our deepest longings and desires, even those which we do not know how to formulate in prayer, and presents them to the Father in a form consistent with God's will in a given situation. Through the intercession of the Holy Spirit, God is answering prayers we don't even know how to make!

God the Father answers our prayers because he has a perfect and loving plan for each of his children; he knows what each of us needs. He uses all things that happen in our lives for his purposes and for our good. Everything that happens to us, even those which seem unfair or bad at the time, can be used by God to teach us, purify us, and draw us close to him.

The Father's ultimate desire, which he fashioned before time began, is that we would become his sons and daughters through faith in Jesus Christ. Through belief in Jesus we become brothers and sisters of Christ, coheirs of the Father's kingdom. In Jesus, we are "predestined," "called," "justified," and "glorified" (Romans 8:29-30). Paul used the past tense in describing God's plan for us, because in Jesus it is already fully completed. Called by God, we have been justified and forgiven of our sins, and glorified by receiving the indwelling Spirit.

These truths should fill us with joy and confidence. We can know that we have the Holy Spirit inside us, guiding us in our efforts to live as Christians and presenting our deepest needs to the Father. For our part, we need to listen closely to the Spirit's promptings, so that we do not act in ways that are contrary to God's will for us.

When situations arise which test our faith, we must ask the Father to show us how they fit into his perfect plan and what he wants to teach us. Most importantly, let us thank the Father each day for calling us to be his children, looking forward to that day when we will be with him forever in heaven.

Romans 8:31-39

³¹ What then shall we say to this? If God is for us, who is against us? ³² He who did not spare his own Son but gave him up for us all, will he not also give us all things with him? ³³ Who shall bring any charge against God's elect? It is God who justifies; ³⁴ who is to condemn? Is it Christ Jesus, who died, yes, who was raised from the dead, who is at the right hand of God, who indeed intercedes for us? ³⁵ Who shall separate us from the love of Christ? Shall tribulation, or distress, or persecution, or famine, or nakedness, or peril, or sword? ³⁶ As it is written,

"For thy sake we are being killed all the day long;
we are regarded as sheep to be slaughtered."

³⁷ No, in all these things we are more than conquerors through him who loved us. ³⁸ For I am sure that neither death, nor life, nor angels, nor principalities, nor things present, nor things to come, nor powers, ³⁹ nor height, nor depth, nor anything else in all creation, will be able to separate us from the love of God in Christ Jesus our Lord.

Paul extolled God's love for us in Jesus Christ. It is clear from his use of imagery that Paul deemed this love crucial for our hope as Christians. There is no compromising: To the extent that we allow God's love to fill us, we will become spiritually strong and unyielding in our faith.

The first issue raised by Paul is God's attitude toward us. Clearly, God is on our side (Romans 8:31-34). Paul insists that there is no condemnation for the believer. Often we are tempted to think that our sins are too great for God to forgive, or that our sinfulness prevents God from loving us. This emphatically is not the case. God the Father himself delivered up Jesus—his only Son—to death on a cross in order that his blood could cleanse us from everything that could keep us from loving and serving God (Hebrews 9:14).

Satan tries to convince us differently. He wants us to believe that we are unloved, even though God has spared nothing in proving his love for us. Jesus is constantly interceding on our behalf so that we will not fall prey to the insidious lies of the evil one.

Paul asks: "Who shall separate us from the love of Christ?" (Romans 8:35). Paul identifies seven difficulties which may beset Christians in varying degrees: hardship, distress, persecution, famine, nakedness, peril, and sword. Christ's love for us is greater and stronger than all of these; it is not diminished or weakened in any way by them. His love for us is our anchor; not our love for him. Our love for God is oftentimes fragile and unreliable. Therefore, it cannot be the standard by which we measure Christ's love for us.

We can confidently trust God's word that nothing can separate us from his love. Indeed, it is often in times of hardship or peril that we experience God's love most deeply because it is in those times that we see our need for him most clearly.

"Lord Jesus, you emptied yourself of everything but love. Love is the very essence of your nature. Fill me today with that love. Help me in times of temptation to remember your cross, and when I do fall, help me to come to you in repentance, renewed and strengthened in your love."

"That Israel May Be Saved"

ROMANS
9:1–11:36

Romans 9:1-5

¹ I am speaking the truth in Christ, I am not lying; my conscience bears me witness in the Holy Spirit, ² that I have great sorrow and unceasing anguish in my heart. ³ For I could wish that I myself were accursed and cut off from Christ for the sake of my brethren, my kinsmen by race. ⁴ They are Israelites, and to them belong the sonship, the glory, the covenants, the giving of the law, the worship, and the promises; ⁵ to them belong the patriarchs, and of their race, according to the flesh, is the Christ. God who is over all be blessed for ever. Amen. ✍

Paul turns now to a discourse on the election of the Israelites and God's great love for them (Romans 9:1–11:36). His words demonstrate a deep longing for his fellow Israelites to accept Jesus as Messiah and know the renewing work of the Holy Spirit.

With his conversion to Christ, Paul experienced growing criticism and rejection by the Jews. Many of them thought he had turned his back on his own people. After all, he was a "Jew, . . . brought up. . . at the feet of Gamaliel, educated according to the strict manner of the law of our fathers, being zealous for God" (Acts 22:3). Precisely because he understood God's call to the Jews, Paul remained zealous for their conversion as well as that of the Gentiles to Christ.

Paul had "great sorrow and unceasing anguish in [his] heart" (Romans 9:2) for the sake of his Jewish brothers and sisters. He even went so far as to say he was willing to be "accursed and cut off from Christ" (9:3) for their sake so that they could participate in the fullness of God's salvation which had been made known and possible by Christ. Paul could not envision a worse fate than to be separated from Christ, but he was willing to accept it for the sake of the Jews. In stating this, he recalled Moses' prayer that he himself be blotted out from the book of life (Exodus 32:32) so that the Israelites might be forgiven.

Paul's deep respect for the work of God in Israel was evident as he wrote of the seven privileges given to the Jews: "sonship, the glory, the covenants, the giving of the law, the worship. . . the promises, and. . . the patriarchs." Most of all, "of their race, according to the flesh, is the Christ" (Romans 9:4-5). He was their greatest privilege and title to glory, even though not recognized as such. Adoption brings to mind the great act of redemption whereby God took the children of Israel as his own: "Israel is my first-born son" (Exodus 4:22). Paul believed that the call to the Gentiles was part of and wholly consistent with that first act of mercy and grace.

Let us respect and love our Jewish brethren whom God called and chose to be his own. May we treasure the work of God in and through them, and pray that God's plan for them will be fulfilled.

Romans 9:6-18

⁶ But it is not as though the word of God had failed. For not all who are descended from Israel belong to Israel, ⁷ and not all are children of Abraham because they are his descendants; but "Through Isaac shall your descendants be named." ⁸ This means that it is not the children of the flesh who are the children of God, but the children of the promise are reckoned as descendants. ⁹ For this is what the promise

said, "About this time I will return and Sarah shall have a son." [10] And not only so, but also when Rebecca had conceived children by one man, our forefather Isaac, [11] though they were not yet born and had done nothing either good or bad, in order that God's purpose of election might continue, not because of works but because of his call, [12] she was told, "The elder will serve the younger." [13] As it is written, "Jacob I loved, but Esau I hated."

[14] What shall we say then? Is there injustice on God's part? By no means! [15] For he says to Moses, "I will have mercy on whom I have mercy, and I will have compassion on whom I have compassion." [16] So it depends not upon man's will or exertion, but upon God's mercy. [17] For the scripture says to Pharaoh, "I have raised you up for the very purpose of showing my power in you, so that my name may be proclaimed in all the earth." [18] So then he has mercy upon whomever he wills, and he hardens the heart of whomever he wills. ✺

The word "mystery" can be overused, but in this reading, Paul truly does confront us with a mystery, with something very difficult to comprehend. At the heart of this mystery is the question of how God's calling for his people, and his purposes for the world, unfold through time. How do we make sense out of some seemingly paradoxical events in salvation history, like the fact that many Jews—God's chosen people—have rejected Christ?

Paul describes some examples which might make us sit back and shake our heads: Not all Abraham's descendants are "true" descendants, but only those born according to the promise, through Isaac—even though Esau, Isaac's firstborn, was rejected by God in favor of his younger brother Jacob. And then there's Pharaoh, who oppressed God's people, yet was allowed to prosper for a time so that God's power could be shown through him. How could God be so unjust and ignore some of the most basic rules of fair play?

The thread which ties these stories together is the mystery of God's mercy: "It depends not upon man's will or exertion, but upon God's mercy. . . . He has mercy upon whomever he wills" (Romans 9:16,18). God's mercy often runs counter to our rational judgments. John's Gospel tells us that we become children of God not through "blood nor of the will of the flesh, nor of the will of man, but of God" (John 1:13). Similarly, John the Baptist reminds the Pharisees that being a son of Abraham is more a matter of the heart than of human descent (Matthew 3:9).

As we reflect on this paradoxical principle of God's mercy, we will come to another conclusion: *Anyone* can receive the mercy of God. It doesn't depend upon us, but upon God, who has shown himself to be merciful to all who call upon him. Since this is the case, we must guard against making snap judgments about individuals or groups of people, even when they seem far from the will of God. Perhaps, even at that moment when we are judging them, God is calling them back to himself. Perhaps he is allowing them to wander far so that they can hear his voice calling them back. Perhaps he wants to show his power through them. Rather than judge or condemn, let us pray that God's mercy comes upon every single person we meet!

"Father, I thank you for your compassion! It is only by your mercy that I am adopted as your child. I want to treasure that mercy at every moment of the day. Help me to intercede so that your mercy falls upon the entire world."

Romans 9:19-33

[19] You will say to me then, "Why does he still find fault? For who can resist his will?" [20] But who are you, a man, to answer back to God? Will what is molded say to its molder, "Why have you made me thus?" [21] Has the potter no right over the clay, to make out of the same lump one vessel for beauty and another for menial use? [22] What if God, desiring to show his wrath and to make known his power, has endured with much patience the vessels of wrath made for destruction, [23] in order to make known the riches of his glory for the vessels of mercy, which he has prepared beforehand for glory, [24] even us whom he has called, not from the Jews only but also from the Gentiles? [25] As indeed he says in Hosea,

"Those who were not my people
I will call 'my people,'
and her who was not beloved
I will call 'my beloved.'"
[26] "And in the very place where it was said to them,
'You are not my people,'
they will be called 'sons of the living God.'"
[27] And Isaiah cries out concerning Israel: "Though the number of the sons of Israel be as the sand of the sea, only a remnant of them will be saved; [28] for the Lord will execute his sentence upon the earth with rigor and dispatch." [29] And as Isaiah predicted,

"If the Lord of hosts had not left us children,
we would have fared like Sodom and been made like Gomorrah."
[30] What shall we say, then? That Gentiles who did not pursue righteousness have attained it, that is, righteousness through faith; [31] but that Israel who pursued the righteousness which is based on law did not succeed in fulfilling that law. [32] Why? Because they did not

pursue it through faith, but as if it were based on works. They have stumbled over the stumbling stone, [33] as it is written,

"Behold, I am laying in Zion a stone that will make men stumble,
a rock that will make them fall;
and he who believes in him will not be put to shame." ☙

W hy did so many Jews reject Jesus while so many Gentiles accepted him? Because righteousness—or the fulfilling of the laws of God—is not based on works, but on faith! Where many Jews held fast to a narrow reading of the Law of Moses, even more Gentiles embraced the message that forgiveness and acceptance by God are possible only because of the cross of Christ.

Does this mean that we need do nothing but passively "believe"? Of course not! Just as Paul talks about *striving* for righteousness by faith, Jesus said that the "work" of God is to believe in him (John 6:29).

Who among us would really doubt that belief is hard work? Every day, we face very real drives and temptations which must be brought into submission to God. Every day, our minds and our wills must be conformed to Christ through obedience to his word. Day in and day out, we face very real choices to say "no" to sinful inclinations, even if we have to look deep within ourselves to confront difficult and deep-seated patterns. By no means is this a passive or easy "work"!

Every day, as we try to listen to the voice of the Holy Spirit, we confront difficulties and choices: How will we react to a touchy situation? Will we give in to a certain weakness? Will we finally say "no" to a temptation that has been bedeviling us? But through it all, we must believe that God is with us and that he wants us to press on and draw closer to him. Here is where our peace and justification lie, in believing that we can be raised up to overcome even our fiercest problems.

When we consider the demands of faith, we might actually want to rely on works instead. It may seem easier to have a list of do's and don'ts which we simply do our best to fulfill. At least then we would be able to control the outcome. But we would also miss so much of God's mercy and forgiveness, and we would never understand how his power is perfected even in our weakness. No wonder Jesus places himself as a stumbling block to such thinking! He wants us to relinquish control of our lives to him so that he can lift us up!

Of course, not all Israelites fell prey to self-righteousness. Look at Mary and Joseph, the disciples, even Nicodemus. And if a Pharisee like Paul can turn to Jesus, what makes us think we're beyond hope?

"Jesus, I want to embrace the work of faith. Help me put aside legalism so that you can transform me!"

Romans 10:1-13

1 Brethren, my heart's desire and prayer to God for them is that they may be saved. 2 I bear them witness that they have a zeal for God, but it is not enlightened. 3 For, being ignorant of the righteousness that comes from God, and seeking to establish their own, they did not submit to God's righteousness. 4 For Christ is the end of the law, that every one who has faith may be justified.

5 Moses writes that the man who practices the righteousness which is based on the law shall live by it. 6 But the righteousness based on faith says, Do not say in your heart, "Who will ascend into heaven?" (that is, to bring Christ down) 7 or "Who will descend into the abyss?" (that is, to bring Christ up from the dead). 8 But what does it

say? The word is near you, on your lips and in your heart (that is, the word of faith which we preach); [9] because, if you confess with your lips that Jesus is Lord and believe in your heart that God raised him from the dead, you will be saved. [10] For man believes with his heart and so is justified, and he confesses with his lips and so is saved. [11] The scripture says, "No one who believes in him will be put to shame." [12] For there is no distinction between Jew and Greek; the same Lord is Lord of all and bestows his riches upon all who call upon him. [13] For, "every one who calls upon the name of the Lord will be saved." ✺

Every one who calls upon the name of the Lord will be saved.
(Romans 10:13)

God wants to save us. He wants to save everyone he has created. Throughout this section of his letter to the Romans (chapters 9-11), Paul has been at great pains to show that this salvation, which God desires for all, depends entirely upon the boundless mercy of our heavenly Father. He chose the Jews as his own people, but they still needed to be saved. He gave them the law and the prophets, to guide them until Christ came, but they still needed Christ. In making these points, Paul was very clear: "Christ is the end of the law, that every one who has faith may be justified" (Romans 10:4).

So what place does the Law of Moses now have? Is it now abolished as an obsolete set of ordinances? No, it is *fulfilled* in Jesus Christ. Every one who believes in him and who accepts his atoning death on the cross is reconciled to God—not by works, nor by observing the law scrupulously, nor by claims to divine election, but by faith in Christ and baptism into his name.

It's not hard for God to save us—or anyone, for that matter! God himself declares: "I will have mercy on whom I have mercy, and I will have compassion on whom I have compassion" (Romans 9:15). Salvation is his mercy and compassion poured out on us. He doesn't say he's going to try really hard, or that he hopes he can do it. No, God the Father states absolutely, positively: "I *will*." Brothers and sisters, if God is so convinced that he can save us, we should be just as eager to accept the salvation he offers. It's not hard to accept; we have only to say, "I will," and trust that God will unfold his marvelous purposes in our lives as we stay close to him!

Do you know beyond doubt that God wants to forgive you today? He wants to deliver you from all bondage, all obstacles, all fears, and all doubts about his power to save and deliver you. He is eager—and powerfully able—to do all good things for you. So, as passionate as he is for us, let us be just as passionate for him!

"I praise you, Father, for sharing your love with me today. I praise you for sending Jesus, so that I can receive your love. Glory to you for enabling me to believe and confess the truth, so that I may be saved and abide in you forever."

Romans 10:14-17

14   But how are men to call upon him in whom they have not believed? And how are they to believe in him of whom they have never heard? And how are they to hear without a preacher? 15 And how can men preach unless they are sent? As it is written, "How beautiful are the feet of those who preach good news!" 16 But they have not all obeyed the gospel; for Isaiah says, "Lord, who has believed

what he has heard from us?" [17] So faith comes from what is heard, and what is heard comes by the preaching of Christ. ✺

How beautiful are the feet of those who preach good news!
(Romans 10:15)

Have you thought about the good news recently? We can be peaceful, even when surrounded by turmoil. We can be healed and freed from the bondage of sin, shame and guilt. We can experience God's tender love as he created us to. We can know God's supreme power in our lives and see it at work in the world every day. We can be confident that our Father will prevail over every challenge to his authority. Why is all this possible? Because Jesus died on the cross and rose from the dead. Because by his blood he initiated a sovereign, unchangeable outpouring of God the Father's love for us.

This is the good news of the gospel—not lofty theological propositions and not a set of rules and regulations handed down from on high. This news is so good that we can sing for the joy of it forever! And we who have heard and embraced this gospel are "sent" (Romans 10:15) to tell others. How can anyone believe in Jesus unless they *hear* (10:14) of the kindness, the mercy, the greatness of what he has done? It's written in Scripture, but it's also written on our hearts. All we have to do is tell people about it. Has Jesus healed you? Comforted you? Forgiven you? Tell someone. Share it. Declare it as fact. Our calling is as simple as that.

For some, that call might entail large, public proclamations. But for most of us, it lies in simple sharing among friends. We don't have to convince, harangue, or scare people into believing the gospel. We have only to believe the message ourselves and tell it as we have experienced it. It needs no embellishment or exaggeration. Sometimes it doesn't even need any words, only the witness of our changed lives.

The good news is so good that it can stand on its own merits. It's so good that it will change the hearts of those around us. Let's allow the Holy Spirit to take care of convincing and convicting people of its truth. The power to transform hearts is God's alone. Ours is simply to "preach the good news."

"Holy Spirit, help me to see where God is working in my life today. Give me opportunities to tell others of your kindness and mercy. And then, gracious Spirit, go to work in their lives, as you have in mine, gently guiding us all as children into the Father's loving embrace."

Romans 10:18-21

18 But I ask, have they not heard? Indeed they have; for
"Their voice has gone out to all the earth,
and their words to the ends of the world.
19 Again I ask, did Israel not understand? First Moses says,
"I will make you jealous of those who are not a nation;
with a foolish nation I will make you angry."
20 Then Isaiah is so bold as to say,
"I have been found by those who did not seek me;
I have shown myself to those who did not ask for me."
21 But of Israel he says, "All day long I have held out my hands to a disobedient and contrary people."

God is so good! No one is beyond the reach of his mercy or the call of his voice. It "has gone out to all the earth, . . . to the ends of the world" (Romans 10:18). And God's limitless mercy is this: "The LORD longs to be gracious to you" (Isaiah 30:18). Even if a mother should forget her child, "yet I will not forget you. Behold, I have graven you on the palms of my hands," says the Lord (49:15-16). "With everlasting love I will have compassion on you" (54:8).

We can never nullify God's love for us, or be outside the reach of his mercy. God says, "I have been found by those who did not seek me; I have shown myself to those who did not ask for me" (Romans 10:20). Indeed, his mercy on us is so great that even "while we were yet sinners, Christ died for us" (5:8). He knew us before we were born (Psalm 139:16) and shed his blood for the sins he knew we'd commit thousands of years after his death!

But God's mercy is not limited to those who accept him. No, he never stopped offering love and salvation to his chosen people, even when they rejected and killed Jesus. And he never will! That is how great his mercy is. "All day long I have held out my hands to a disobedient and contrary people" (Romans 10:21). His hands do not tire, nor does his patience fail.

Is there a sin you feel weighed down by, something that you try to overcome, only to fall again and again? Bring it to the Lord in prayer, in the sacrament of Reconciliation. It is not beyond God's mercy to forgive and heal. Do you know someone you believe to be outside the reach of God's touch? Pray and intercede for them! God can and will touch them—today, tomorrow, in ten years, in his own time. His mercy goes out to the ends of the world.

"Holy Spirit, fill me with hope in God's mercy. Help me be courageous in facing my need for it, and persevering in prayer for others. Let my voice be one that declares the Father's love and mercy, today and always."

Romans 11:1-12

[1] I ask, then, has God rejected his people? By no means! I myself am an Israelite, a descendant of Abraham, a member of the tribe of Benjamin. [2] God has not rejected his people whom he foreknew. Do you not know what the scripture says of Elijah, how he pleads with God against Israel? [3] "Lord, they have killed your prophets, they have demolished your altars, and I alone am left, and they seek my life." [4] But what is God's reply to him? "I have kept for myself seven thousand men who have not bowed the knee to Baal." [5] So too at the present time there is a remnant, chosen by grace. [6] But if it is by grace, it is no longer on the basis of works; otherwise grace would no longer be grace.

[7] What then? Israel failed to obtain what it sought. The elect obtained it, but the rest were hardened, [8] as it is written,

"God gave them a spirit of stupor,

eyes that should not see and ears that should not hear,

down to this very day."

[9] And David says,

"Let their table become a snare and a trap,

a pitfall and a retribution for them;

[10] let their eyes be darkened so that they cannot see, and bend their backs for ever."

[11] So I ask, have they stumbled so as to fall? By no means! But through their trespass salvation has come to the Gentiles, so as to

make Israel jealous. [12] Now if their trespass means riches for the world, and if their failure means riches for the Gentiles, how much more will their full inclusion mean! ↷

Has God rejected his people? By no means! (Romans 11:1)

How often do we consider the important and royal place of the Jews in salvation history? It was through the Jews that we received not only God's commandments and promises, but also salvation itself. We are right to believe that we are chosen by grace, but very mistaken if we think our place in God's kingdom nullifies the covenants he has made with his chosen ones. "God has not rejected his people whom he foreknew" (Romans 11:2). "For the LORD will not forsake his people; he will not abandon his heritage" (Psalm 94:14).

The Israelites, "though well attested by their faith, did not receive what was promised, since God had foreseen something better for us, that apart from us they should not be made perfect" (Hebrews 11:39-40). Throughout the Old Testament, we read about God dispersing his chosen ones for times of refining, but always bringing them back with love. The Israelites have indeed paid a high price for being God's chosen. He has held them to a higher degree of holiness. Time and again we see them humbled and broken. And, time and again we see God receiving them back with merciful love.

Even with the advent of Christianity, the Jews have remained an object of persecution. The past century alone witnessed the greatest attempt to obliterate them under Nazi persecution. Yet, not only did the Holocaust fail to achieve its goal, it brought the Jewish people back to the promised land and reestablished Israel as a sovereign nation after centuries of exile. God fulfilled his promise: "I will. . . gather you from all the countries, and bring you into your own land" (Ezekiel 36:24).

Israel's history should challenge us to examine whether prejudice or indifference characterizes our attitude toward God's chosen people. Our respect for them should be great indeed, considering all they have given us. Let us repent of any sinful thinking and pray that our Jewish brothers and sisters might enjoy the fullness of the covenant that God has provided.

"Lord, may you bless your people along with us. We place your name on the people of Israel. May your grace continue to be upon all of us, and may your peace be upon Jerusalem."

Romans 11:13-24

[13] Now I am speaking to you Gentiles. Inasmuch then as I am an apostle to the Gentiles, I magnify my ministry [14] in order to make my fellow Jews jealous, and thus save some of them. [15] For if their rejection means the reconciliation of the world, what will their acceptance mean but life from the dead? [16] If the dough offered as first fruits is holy, so is the whole lump; and if the root is holy, so are the branches.
[17] But if some of the branches were broken off, and you, a wild olive shoot, were grafted in their place to share the richness of the olive tree, [18] do not boast over the branches. If you do boast, remember it is not you that support the root, but the root that supports you.
[19] You will say, "Branches were broken off so that I might be grafted in."
[20] That is true. They were broken off because of their unbelief, but you stand fast only through faith. So do not become proud, but stand in

awe. [21] For if God did not spare the natural branches, neither will he spare you. [22] Note then the kindness and the severity of God: severity toward those who have fallen, but God's kindness to you, provided you continue in his kindness; otherwise you too will be cut off. [23] And even the others, if they do not persist in their unbelief, will be grafted in, for God has the power to graft them in again. [24] For if you have been cut from what is by nature a wild olive tree, and grafted, contrary to nature, into a cultivated olive tree, how much more will these natural branches be grafted back into their own olive tree.

We may not all be farmers, but the image of being "grafted" can still speak as powerfully to us as it did to the believers in first-century Rome. Winding up his discussion of the mystery of why so many of his fellow Jews had rejected the gospel, Paul wanted to make sure that the gentile Christians in Rome would not become proud or boastful. Just as Jewish rejection is a mystery of God's purposes, so too is gentile inclusion. In other words, no one can take credit for his or her faith. It is the fruit of the Spirit's work within us, not primarily of our own actions and decisions.

How does this speak to us today? We all believe that at baptism, we were grafted into Christ Jesus: We who are created were joined to the uncreated God; we who are fallen were joined to our all-perfect and holy Lord. Since this is the case, it is no wonder that the purity of the life of Christ can seem alien to us. We shouldn't be surprised by the difficulties and challenges we face as we strive to turn from sin and develop godly habits.

However, we should never conclude that, since our nature can seem so contrary to the "rich root system" into which we have been grafted, we will never truly resemble the Lord. Realizing our short-falls should never lead us to despair. The "grafting" itself is a work of grace, and if we want to become one with Jesus, we must learn to rely on his Spirit to continue the work he began when we were bap-tized.

Just as a new branch grafted into a tree will not survive if it does not draw nourishment from the root, we will grow in our life with Christ to the extent that we draw life from him. As we continue to obey the commandments and submit to the Spirit, we will receive more life from our "root," which is Christ. And as more of the divine life flows to us, we will become more like him.

We may not like to hear Paul's words of caution, "It is not you that support the root, but the root that supports you. . . . You stand fast only through faith" (Romans 11:18,20). But upon reflection, these words can be a great comfort to us. Jesus himself supports us, and through faith in him and the power of his cross, we can receive everything we need to stand firm!

"Holy Spirit, flow through me with the life of Christ! I want to be a fruitful branch, allowing the grace of God to transform my nat-ural inclinations so that I resemble Christ!"

Romans 11:25-36

25 Lest you be wise in your own conceits, I want you to understand this mystery, brethren: a hardening has come upon part of Israel, until the full number of the Gentiles come in, 26 and so all Israel will be saved; as it is written,

"The Deliverer will come from Zion,

he will banish ungodliness from Jacob";

27 "and this will be my covenant with them

when I take away their sins."

28 As regards the gospel they are enemies of God, for your sake; but as regards election they are beloved for the sake of their forefathers. 29 For the gifts and the call of God are irrevocable. 30 Just as you were once disobedient to God but now have received mercy because of their disobedience, 31 so they have now been disobedient in order that by the mercy shown to you they also may receive mercy. 32 For God has consigned all men to disobedience, that he may have mercy upon all.

33 O the depth of the riches and wisdom and knowledge of God! How unsearchable are his judgments and how inscrutable his ways!

34 "For who has known the mind of the Lord, or who has been his counselor?"

35 "Or who has given a gift to him that he might be repaid?"

36 For from him and through him and to him are all things. To him be glory for ever. Amen.

Even though most of his fellow Jews had not accepted Jesus as the Messiah, Paul knew that they were still God's beloved (Romans 11:28) and that God would never take away the gifts he had lavished upon them or the call he had given them (11:29). Paul also realized that God was using the Jews to bring other people and nations to himself (11:25). Finally, although Paul could not grasp exactly how— God's ways are so unsearchable and inscrutable (11:33)—he believed that God's chosen people will ultimately turn to him and know his salvation (11:26).

History has shown us that not all Christians have fully embraced Paul's teaching and attitude toward the Jewish people. In fact, too many times people have twisted Paul's words and used them as justification for persecution against the Jews. During his pilgrimage to the Holy Land in Jubilee Year 2000, Pope John Paul II visited Yad Vashem Holocaust Memorial and offered these words of peace and reconciliation to his Jewish brothers and sisters:

Jews and Christians share an immense spiritual patrimony, flowing from God's self-revelation. Our religious teachings and our spiritual experience demand that we overcome evil with good. . . . Only a world at peace, with justice for all, can avoid repeating the mistakes and terrible crimes of the past.

As bishop of Rome and successor of the Apostle Peter, I assure the Jewish people that the Catholic Church, motivated by the gospel law of truth and love, and by no political considerations, is deeply saddened by the hatred, acts of persecution and displays of anti-Semitism directed against the Jews by Christians at any time and in any place.

The church rejects racism in any form as a denial of the image of the Creator inherent in every human being.

In this place of solemn remembrance, I fervently pray that our sorrow for the tragedy which the Jewish people suffered in the twentieth century will lead to a new relationship between Christians and Jews. Let us build a new future in which there will be no more anti-Jewish feeling among Christians or anti-Christian feeling among Jews, but rather the mutual respect required of those who adore the one Creator and Lord, and look to Abraham as our common father in faith.

And at Judaism's holiest site, the Western Wall, the Holy Father prayed to God and again asked Jews to forgive centuries of Christian sins against their people:

> We are deeply saddened by the behavior of those who in the course of history have caused these children of yours to suffer and, asking your forgiveness, we wish to commit ourselves to genuine brotherhood with the people of the Covenant.

In this same spirit of repentance, let us all pray together that the path may be smoothed before them for God's beloved people to turn to his Son, Jesus the Messiah.

Transformed by Grace

ROMANS
12:1–15:13

Romans 12:1-8

[1] I appeal to you therefore, brethren, by the mercies of God, to present your bodies as a living sacrifice, holy and acceptable to God, which is your spiritual worship. [2] Do not be conformed to this world but be transformed by the renewal of your mind, that you may prove what is the will of God, what is good and acceptable and perfect. [3] For by the grace given to me I bid every one among you not to think of himself more highly than he ought to think, but to think with sober judgment, each according to the measure of faith which God has assigned him. [4] For as in one body we have many members, and all the members do not have the same function, [5] so we, though many, are one body in Christ, and individually members one of another. [6] Having gifts that differ according to the grace given to us, let us use them: if prophecy, in proportion to our faith; [7] if service, in our serving; he who teaches, in his teaching; [8] he who exhorts, in his exhortation; he who contributes, in liberality; he who gives aid, with zeal; he who does acts of mercy, with cheerfulness. ✍

Under the Mosaic Law, the Jews sacrificed animals in the temple as acts of worship to God. Now, through the new covenant in Christ, the way of worshipping and offering sacrifice to God has changed. As Christians, we give "spiritual worship" to God by presenting ourselves—body and mind—to him as a "living sacrifice." As St. Irenaeus once observed, God is most fully worshipped and glorified when his people are most fully alive in him.

This is why Paul urged the Romans to be careful not to adapt themselves to the standards and customs of the world around them.

He knew that if they did, they would no longer be fully alive in Christ, and as a result God would be robbed of the worship he deserved. Rather, Paul urged them to allow the new mind they received in baptism to transform the way they lived. Then, God would be glorified by the witness of those who believe in him.

What does it mean to be transformed by a renewed mind? It means letting the Holy Spirit teach us to think in a whole new way. God wants to do more than just pardon our sin. He wants to "renovate" us from the inside out. He wants to change our attitudes and give us a fresh way of thinking, so we can take our eyes off ourselves and live as members of one body, helping each other on the way to salvation.

Do you believe that you are linked with every other member of the church of Christ (Romans 12:4-5)? This is one of the central truths that the Spirit wants to teach us as he renews our minds. We all share a responsibility for one another: The way we behave toward each other can help all of us reflect God's image. Or we can be instrumental in moving other people farther away from that image. As the well-known Christian apologist C. S. Lewis once pointed out, "All day long we are, in some degree, helping each other to one or other of these destinations."

How can we tell we are being renewed? By the degree to which we find ourselves thinking and acting as members of the body of Christ. By the degree to which we find ourselves relying on other Christians for support and encouragement, and serving them freely and eagerly. Taking time to encourage the depressed or broken-hearted, giving cheerfully and generously to someone in need, loving beyond our "natural inclinations"—these are all concrete signs that God is transforming us.

"Come, Holy Spirit, and open my eyes so that I can see where you are working in my life to transform and renew me. Help me to cooperate with this 'renovation.' Have your way with me, for I am yours."

Romans 12:9-21

9 Let love be genuine; hate what is evil, hold fast to what is good; 10 love one another with brotherly affection; outdo one another in showing honor. 11 Never flag in zeal, be aglow with the Spirit, serve the Lord. 12 Rejoice in your hope, be patient in tribulation, be constant in prayer. 13 Contribute to the needs of the saints, practice hospitality.

14 Bless those who persecute you; bless and do not curse them. 15 Rejoice with those who rejoice, weep with those who weep. 16 Live in harmony with one another; do not be haughty, but associate with the lowly; never be conceited. 17 Repay no one evil for evil, but take thought for what is noble in the sight of all. 18 If possible, so far as it depends upon you, live peaceably with all. 19 Beloved, never avenge yourselves, but leave it to the wrath of God; for it is written, "Vengeance is mine, I will repay, says the Lord." 20 No, "if your enemy is hungry, feed him; if he is thirsty, give him drink; for by so doing you will heap burning coals upon his head." 21 Do not be overcome by evil, but overcome evil with good. ⤸

At the opening of chapter 12 Paul urged the Romans to make a "holy and acceptable" sacrifice of themselves to God (Romans 12:1). In order to do that, he told them, they must learn to recognize God's will and live according to it instead of conforming to worldly ways (12:2). In other words, the Roman Christians were to reflect God's righteousness in the concrete ways they lived their lives. Now, Paul's clear and specific directives in verses 9-21 show us all how to do this.

As diverse as Paul's exhortations may seem—there are nearly thirty of them, packed into thirteen short verses—each one points toward the same end: a life lived according to God's love, a love which permeates everything we say and think and do. All of Paul's exhortations have to do with maintaining our unity and caring for one another as if we were members of the same body.

This is not abstract theology. Paul's directions are far from "ethereal" or "otherworldly." They are, on the contrary, quite practical and down-to-earth! "Love one another with brotherly affection." "Outdo one another in showing honor." "Contribute to the needs of the saints." "Bless those who persecute you." "Live in harmony with one another" (Romans 12:10,13,14,16). When you help out at the local homeless shelter, when you comfort a grieving friend, even when you simply smile warmly at someone who seems depressed or lonely, you are putting Paul's advice into practice. When you are patient with your coworkers today, when you resist speaking against or getting back at someone who has wronged you, you are actually giving *spiritual worship* to God. Why? Because you're conforming to his will and loving others as he has loved you.

If Paul's exhortations sound too challenging, remember what he has been saying all throughout this letter: We have been saved by God's grace through faith in Jesus. We have died to sin. Jesus Christ lives in us. We are being renewed by the Holy Spirit. When we know and believe all this, we can live the life of love that Paul describes, for "God's love has been poured into our hearts through the Holy Spirit which has been given to us" (Romans 5:5).

Romans 13:1-7

[1] Let every person be subject to the governing authorities. For there is no authority except from God, and those that exist have been instituted by God. [2] Therefore he who resists the authorities resists what God has appointed, and those who resist will incur judgment. [3] For rulers are not a terror to good conduct, but to bad. Would you have no fear of him who is in authority? Then do what is good, and you will receive his approval, [4] for he is God's servant for your good. But if you do wrong, be afraid, for he does not bear the sword in vain; he is the servant of God to execute his wrath on the wrongdoer. [5] Therefore one must be subject, not only to avoid God's wrath but also for the sake of conscience.[6] For the same reason you also pay taxes, for the authorities are ministers of God, attending to this very thing. [7] Pay all of them their dues, taxes to whom taxes are due, revenue to whom revenue is due, respect to whom respect is due, honor to whom honor is due.

Paul spent a lot of effort in his letter to the Romans telling them that they were not under the burden of the law. "Well, then, do we still have to pay taxes and obey the government?" these Christians who lived in a great empire may have wondered. A clear "yes" would be Paul's answer to such a question, for, he explained, "authorities are ministers of God" (Romans 13:6). So, he would add, "pay all of them their dues, taxes to whom taxes are due, revenue to whom revenue is due, respect to whom respect is due, honor to whom honor is due" (13:7).

In such a brief letter Paul couldn't address complex issues concerning the exercise of power in a way contrary to moral order, the violation of the fundamental rights of the human person and other questions of conscience that Christians may encounter from the civil government. He did, however, clearly affirm that God instituted political authority for the well-being of society (Romans 13:1,4), even if that authority is sometimes misused or abused.

Christian freedom does not eliminate the debt of obedience to civil authorities which are intended to serve society's common good. Thus, believers cannot live lawlessly nor can they neglect their civil obligations such as obeying just laws and paying taxes— and voting, Paul might add if he were writing today—for these responsibilities are ordained by God. In addition, we should pray for our government leaders and elected officials, that they govern wisely and justly and "that we may lead a quiet and peaceable life, godly and respectful in every way" (1 Timothy 2:2).

St. Peter wrote the same message as Paul did: "Be subject for the Lord's sake to every human institution. . . . Live as free men, yet without using your freedom as a pretext for evil; but live as servants of God" (1 Peter 2:13,16). Building on the teaching of the apostles, the *Catechism of the Catholic Church* declares:

It is the duty of citizens to contribute along with the civil authorities to the good of society in a spirit of truth, justice, solidarity, and freedom. The love and service of one's country follow from the duty of gratitude and belong to the order of charity. Submission to legitimate authorities and service of the common good require citizens to fulfill their roles in the life of the political community. (CCC, 2239)

"Father, guide those who govern our nation and those who live under its authority. Help us all to follow the ways of justice, peace, and righteousness."

Romans 13:8-10

[8] Owe no one anything, except to love one another; for he who loves his neighbor has fulfilled the law. [9] The commandments, "You shall not commit adultery, You shall not kill, You shall not steal, You shall not covet," and any other commandment, are summed up in this sentence, "You shall love your neighbor as yourself." [10] Love does no wrong to a neighbor; therefore love is the fulfilling of the law.

*Owe no one anything, except to love one another; for he who loves his
neighbor has fulfilled the law. (Romans 13:8)*

J esus, who brought justification and salvation to all believers,
taught that loving others fulfills the law. He healed the man
with a withered hand even though it broke the Sabbath law
because he knew that it is better to do good than to do harm by
adhering to convention (Mark 3:1-5). One of the scribes summed
up Jesus' teaching: We are "to love [God] with all the heart, and
with all the understanding, and with all the strength, and to love
one's neighbor as oneself" (12:33). Paul echoed Jesus' teaching:
"The commandments. . . are summed up in this sentence, 'You shall
love your neighbor as yourself'" (Romans 13:9).

Paul wanted the Roman Christians (who were mostly Gentile with
a Judeo-Christian minority) to understand that God has called all people to be his children. He wants everyone to partake of eternal
life—not just those in the community of faith. Once the Romans came
to understand that all people are loved by God and called to be his children, Paul's hope was that they would set aside their differences and
love each other.

Christ was "the end of the law" (Romans 10:4). His death on the
cross was the ultimate act of love that established a new norm for
Christian living, enabling us to be freed from the bonds of convic-
tion, nationality, ethnicity, and race to seek more actively the good
for others. When we accept Christ's love, we are united with him in
his death and resurrection. We are empowered through love to lay
our lives down for others as Christ did for us.

Those who live in the isolation of today's Western societies may
think God's call to love our neighbor is an impossible task.
Humanly it is impossible, but God has made it possible by giving us

his Holy Spirit, through whom his "love has been poured into our hearts" (Romans 5:5). The Holy Spirit enables us to "put on the Lord Jesus Christ" (13:14) and to love as Christ loved.

Let us pray with Paul: "May the God of steadfastness and encouragement grant [us] to live in harmony with one another, in accord with Christ Jesus, that together [we] may with one voice glorify the God and Father of our Lord Jesus Christ" (Romans 15:5-6).

Romans 13:11-14

[11] Besides this you know what hour it is, how it is full time now for you to wake from sleep. For salvation is nearer to us now than when we first believed; [12] the night is far gone, the day is at hand. Let us then cast off the works of darkness and put on the armor of light; [13] let us conduct ourselves becomingly as in the day, not in reveling and drunkenness, not in debauchery and licentiousness, not in quarreling and jealousy. [14] But put on the Lord Jesus Christ, and make no provision for the flesh, to gratify its desires. ✍

Frequently infants are dressed in a white christening gown for their baptism. In the Rite of Christian Initiation for Adults (RCIA) the newly baptized may be given a white baptismal garment. These white robes remind us that the baptized have "put on" Christ.

In an exhortation addressed to newly baptized Christians, St. Augustine recalled Paul's words to the Romans:

*Put on the Lord Jesus Christ, and make no provision for the flesh
and its desires,* so that you may be clothed with the life of him
whom you have put on in this sacrament. . . . It is a sacrament
of new life which begins here and now with the forgiveness of
all past sins, and will be brought to completion in the resurrection of the dead. *You have been buried with Christ by baptism
into death, in order that, as Christ has risen from the dead, you also
may walk in newness of life.* (Sermon 8, Octave of Easter)

It was, in fact, after reading Paul's words "Put on the Lord Jesus
Christ, and make no provision for the flesh, to gratify its desires"
(Romans 13:14), that Augustine, who had long been caught up in
immorality and spiritual lethargy, finally cast off his sinful ways and
embraced the faith. "I read no further nor was there any need to,"
he later wrote about his conversion, "for with the end of this sentence, as by a clear and constant light infused into my heart, the
darkness of all former doubts was immediately driven away"
(*Confessions*, VII, 12, 29).

Every baptized Christian is called to live in the life and power of
the risen Christ. The day of the resurrection—the new creation—
has already dawned for us, even while the night of sin continues
around us. Paul wrote with an urgency—"it is full time now for you
to wake from sleep . . . the night is far gone, the day is at hand" —
calling believers to cast off the works of darkness and walk in the
light of day (Romans 13:11-13). May each of us bring our baptismal
garment "unstained into the everlasting life of heaven" (Rite of
Baptism). As we have "put on Christ," may we be transformed day
by day to be more like him, shining as his lights in the world.

Romans 14:1-12

1 As for the man who is weak in faith, welcome him, but not for disputes over opinions. 2 One believes he may eat anything, while the weak man eats only vegetables. 3 Let not him who eats despise him who abstains, and let not him who abstains pass judgment on him who eats; for God has welcomed him. 4 Who are you to pass judgment on the servant of another? It is before his own master that he stands or falls. And he will be upheld, for the Master is able to make him stand.

5 One man esteems one day as better than another, while another man esteems all days alike. Let every one be fully convinced in his own mind. 6 He who observes the day, observes it in honor of the Lord. He also who eats, eats in honor of the Lord, since he gives thanks to God; while he who abstains, abstains in honor of the Lord and gives thanks to God. 7 None of us lives to himself, and none of us dies to himself. 8 If we live, we live to the Lord, and if we die, we die to the Lord; so then, whether we live or whether we die, we are the Lord's. 9 For to this end Christ died and lived again, that he might be Lord both of the dead and of the living.

10 Why do you pass judgment on your brother? Or you, why do you despise your brother? For we shall all stand before the judgment seat of God; 11 for it is written,

"As I live, says the Lord, every knee shall bow to me,
and every tongue shall give praise to God."

12 So each of us shall give account of himself to God.

P aul took up the problem of being judgmental in his letter to the Romans. It seems that the stronger in faith were sometimes passing judgment on their weaker brothers and sisters. In order to deal with this, Paul reminded his readers that Jesus is the only Lord and Judge. In addition, Paul exhorted the Romans always to treat their weaker brothers and sisters with compassion to help them to grow in their Christian lives.

Jesus is *Kyrios*, the Lord and the ruler of the universe. We are under his authority in this life as well as when we die. "So then, whether we live or whether we die, we are the Lord's" (Romans 14:8). We will be judged as to how we have obeyed God's commandment to love our neighbors. Jesus ransomed us from captivity to sin. We are now free to submit willingly to Jesus Christ as our Lord and Savior. Paul's point was that it was more important to recognize that we are subject to Christ's judgment than it is to judge others.

Parents and pastors, and all those who are trying to lead people to Jesus, are probably familiar with the frustrations that are sometimes associated with helping new Christians to grow in their faith, to break the grip of their former ways of life. To all these people, Paul's message resonates with these words: *Be compassionate.*

In the Gospel of Matthew, Jesus spoke of the danger of pointing out the speck in the eye of one's neighbor while ignoring the log in one's own (Matthew 7:3). Jesus accepts all those who sincerely give their lives to him, who try to repent of their sins and grow stronger in their faith. So too must we. We are called to love, correct, and admonish our brothers and sisters, but the goal must always be their growth and edification, not their embarrassment or humiliation.

"Jesus, you are my Lord and Savior and I commit myself to serving and obeying you. Give me the grace to love my brothers and sisters, to encourage them, and to accept their encouragement in living out the Christian life. May I never judge unjustly, but follow you in your way of love and justice, so that you may use me to bring others to you."

Romans 14:13-23

13   Then let us no more pass judgment on one another, but rather decide never to put a stumbling block or hindrance in the way of a brother. [14] I know and am persuaded in the Lord Jesus that nothing is unclean in itself; but it is unclean for any one who thinks it unclean. [15] If your brother is being injured by what you eat, you are no longer walking in love. Do not let what you eat cause the ruin of one for whom Christ died. [16] So do not let your good be spoken of as evil. [17] For the kingdom of God is not food and drink but righteousness and peace and joy in the Holy Spirit; [18] he who thus serves Christ is acceptable to God and approved by men. [19] Let us then pursue what makes for peace and for mutual upbuilding. [20] Do not, for the sake of food, destroy the work of God. Everything is indeed clean, but it is wrong for any one to make others fall by what he eats; [21] it is right not to eat meat or drink wine or do anything that makes your brother stumble. [22] The faith that you have, keep between yourself and God; happy is he who has no reason to judge himself for what he approves. [23] But he who has doubts is condemned, if he eats, because he does not act from faith; for whatever does not proceed from faith is sin.

U nity in essentials, freedom in doubtful matters, and in all things charity." This traditional motto of the church sums up Paul's exhortation in chapter 14 well. Paul cautioned the Romans not to pass judgment on others and not to put a hindrance in another's way because of what different members of the community ate. Those Jewish Christians who held to the Mosaic Law considered certain foods unclean and refrained from eating them. Moreover, they were scandalized by others who disregarded these dietary restrictions. At the same time, those who in freedom of spirit ate whatever they wanted looked down on the others as "weak" and seemed to have no problem in making their opinions known. That's why Paul admonished them: "You are no longer walking in love" (Romans 14:15).

We may no longer be troubled by this particular issue. After all, we know that Jesus has freed us from the obligation to fulfill the dietary regulations of the Mosaic code. Yet Paul's words still hold good as a principle that can be applied to many other arenas: Our freedom in Christ does not entitle us to ignore the demands of love.

How often have you dug in your heels on some matter of little importance just because you wanted your own way? It can be deceptively easy to hold on to our own perspective and remain unyielding toward those whose outlook differs from ours. Or we might consider our position "right" and label those who think or act differently "wrong." This sort of behavior divides people from one another. Such inflexible attitudes only leave hurt feelings, resentment, and disunity in their wake. Paul warned, "Do not, for the sake of food, destroy the work of God" (Romans 14:20). We might also take his words as a warning against satisfying our whims or promoting our opinions on issues of minor consequence.

Instead of judging other people, let's allow love to guide us as we make every effort to preserve unity and peace in our family, in our community, in our parish, and in the whole Christian church. This may, at times, mean putting aside our own interests, suffering inconveniences, or sacrificing our preferences in order to maintain unity and harmony. It might be necessary to adjust our own actions and beliefs in lesser matters to build up and strengthen our neighbor's faith rather than undermine it. And in the end, isn't that the heart of Christian love and fellowship?

"Father, help me to 'pursue what makes for peace and for mutual upbuilding' (Romans 14:19). Widen my heart so that I can learn to love and respect those who are not just like me in every way."

Romans 15:1-13

1   We who are strong ought to bear with the failings of the weak, and not to please ourselves; 2 let each of us please his neighbor for his good, to edify him. 3 For Christ did not please himself; but, as it is written, "The reproaches of those who reproached thee fell on me." 4 For whatever was written in former days was written for our instruction, that by steadfastness and by the encouragement of the scriptures we might have hope. 5 May the God of steadfastness and encouragement grant you to live in such harmony with one another, in accord with Christ Jesus, 6 that together you may with one voice glorify the God and Father of our Lord Jesus Christ.

7   Welcome one another, therefore, as Christ has welcomed you, for the glory of God. 8 For I tell you that Christ became a servant to the circumcised to show God's truthfulness, in order to confirm the promises given to the patriarchs, 9 and in order that the Gentiles might glorify God for his mercy. As it is written,

"Therefore I will praise thee among the Gentiles,
and sing to thy name";
10 and again it is said,
"Rejoice, O Gentiles, with his people";
11 and again,
"Praise the Lord, all Gentiles,
and let all the peoples praise him";
12 and further Isaiah says,
"The root of Jesse shall come,
he who rises to rule the Gentiles;
in him shall the Gentiles hope."
13 May the God of hope fill you with all joy and peace in believing, so
that by the power of the Holy Spirit you may abound in hope.

P aul's great desire for the Romans was that they all live in harmony with each other. In order to achieve this goal, he encouraged those among them who were stronger in their faith to bear
with the failings of the weak (Romans 15:1). In addition, he urged all
members of the community to welcome one another as Christ had welcomed each of them, Jew and Gentile alike (15:7), and to serve one
another because Christ had become a servant himself for their sake
(15:8). In brief, Paul's various bits of practical advice all focused on
mutual love and service as the foundation for unity and harmony. It
was charity toward one another that was to rule among all the members of the Christian church in Rome and unite them.

Paul's appeal to the first-century Romans to live in love and unity
reaches out to Christians in all places and in every age. But this may
seem very challenging to us when we read his appeal today. "How can

I get along with that irritating parish committee member who sees and thinks about everything so differently than I do?" "What should I do about that neighbor of mine who insists on bending my ear every time he sees me?" "How much more help can my sister possibly want from me?" Fortunately, Paul added another bit of advice: We are "not to please ourselves; let each of us please his neighbor for his good, to edify him. For Christ did not please himself" (Romans 15:1-3).

Dying on the cross certainly wasn't something Jesus did to please himself. His love was sacrificial, not self-centered or self-seeking. As he told his disciples, "Whoever would be great among you must be your servant, and whoever would be first among you must be slave of all. For the Son of man also came not to be served but to serve" (Mark 10:45).

God has poured his love into our hearts through the Holy Spirit (Romans 5:8). We can rely on his Spirit to help us put others first and to love them freely and serve them wholeheartedly as Christ did. As we do, Paul's prayer for the Romans will be fulfilled in us, too: "May the God of steadfastness and encouragement grant you to live in such harmony with one another, in accord with Christ Jesus, that together you may with one voice glorify the God and Father of our Lord Jesus Christ" (15:5-6).

"May the God of Peace Be with You"

ROMANS
15:14–16:27

Romans 15:14-21

[14] I myself am satisfied about you, my brethren, that you yourselves are full of goodness, filled with all knowledge, and able to instruct one another. [15] But on some points I have written to you very boldly by way of reminder, because of the grace given me by God [16] to be a minister of Christ Jesus to the Gentiles in the priestly service of the gospel of God, so that the offering of the Gentiles may be acceptable, sanctified by the Holy Spirit. [17] In Christ Jesus, then, I have reason to be proud of my work for God. [18] For I will not venture to speak of anything except what Christ has wrought through me to win obedience from the Gentiles, by word and deed, [19] by the power of signs and wonders, by the power of the Holy Spirit, so that from Jerusalem and as far round as Illyricum I have fully preached the gospel of Christ, [20] thus making it my ambition to preach the gospel, not where Christ has already been named, lest I build on another man's foundation, [21] but as it is written,

"They shall see who have never been told of him,
and they shall understand who have never heard of him." 〜

How did St. Paul look upon his ministry to the Gentiles? How did he recognize the great responsibility that God had given him in this matter, and how was he faithful to this mandate? Paul used the word *leitourgos* (Romans 15:16), which is translated as "minister" to describe his God-given charge. Through his use of the word *leitourgos*, Paul stressed that his preaching was like a liturgical ministry. In other words, when he preached, he was functioning like a priest in the sanctuary. Paul added that he dared not speak of anything except what Christ had done through him with mighty signs and marvels, and with the power of the Holy Spirit (15:18-19).

From Paul's words, we can make three observations about how Christians minister to Christ Jesus. First, we should regard the call to proclaim the gospel as truly important (Romans 15:16-17). God calls some to the ordained ministry as deacons, priests, or ministers, but by virtue of our baptism, all Christians are members of the priesthood of the faithful. As such, Christ asks us to share the good news. In carrying out this important task, we are ministering to the people and serving God's sanctuary.

Second, when we share the good news, we should follow Paul's example by speaking of what God has done through us (Romans 15:18). The first step in an effective proclamation of the gospel is that we recognize and acknowledge God's work in our lives. The reality of God's work in our lives will give credibility to our words. This will not be the case if we speak about the gospel when we, in fact, do not know its effects in our own lives.

Finally, Paul expected signs and wonders to occur and the power of the Spirit to be released when he proclaimed the gospel (Romans 15:19). We can imitate this attitude and expect the power of God to be made manifest when we share the gospel. God is, after all, behind the work he does in us and through us.

"Lord Jesus, I desire to be your minister in the work of sharing the good news of salvation in you. May the Spirit teach me to reverence the work of God and to expect heaven to visit earth as I proclaim your holy name and work."

Romans 15:22-33

22 This is the reason why I have so often been hindered from coming to you. 23 But now, since I no longer have any room for work in these regions, and since I have longed for many years to come to you, 24 I hope to see you in passing as I go to Spain, and to be sped on my journey there by you, once I have enjoyed your company for a little. 25 At present, however, I am going to Jerusalem with aid for the saints. 26 For Macedonia and Achaia have been pleased to make some contribution for the poor among the saints at Jerusalem; 27 they were pleased to do it, and indeed they are in debt to them, for if the Gentiles have come to share in their spiritual blessings, they ought also to be of service to them in material blessings. 28 When therefore I have completed this, and have delivered to them what has been raised, I shall go on by way of you to Spain; 29 and I know that when I come to you I shall come in the fullness of the blessing of Christ.

30 I appeal to you, brethren, by our Lord Jesus Christ and by the love of the Spirit, to strive together with me in your prayers to God on my behalf, 31 that I may be delivered from the unbelievers in Judea, and that my service for Jerusalem may be acceptable to the saints, 32 so that by God's will I may come to you with joy and be refreshed in your company. 33 The God of peace be with you all. Amen.

Catholic with a small "c" means universal, or all-embracing. Thus, as the *Catechism of the Catholic Church* explains, the church is catholic in a double sense:

> First, the church is catholic because Christ is present in her . . . . In her subsists the fullness of Christ's body united with its head; this implies that she receives from him 'the fullness of the means of salvation'. . . The church was, in this fundamental sense, catholic on the day of Pentecost and will always be so. (CCC, 830)

In another sense, the church is catholic because she has been sent out by Christ on a mission to the whole human race:

> All men are called to belong to the new People of God. This People, therefore, while remaining one and only one, is to be spread throughout the whole world and to all ages in order that the design of God's will may be fulfilled. (CCC, 831)

Paul's ministry and travels reflect just how catholic the church has been from its earliest days. As he explained to the Roman Christians, Paul had not yet been able to visit them because he had been preaching in so many other regions (Romans 15:22). Now he intended to see them on his way to Spain (15:24,28), another land where he hoped to proclaim the gospel. But first he planned to go to Jerusalem to deliver money which the Christians in Macedonia and Achaia had donated to help the Jerusalem church, which was struggling through a famine (15:25-26). These few verses highlight how closely the early Christians—in spite of differences in nationality, language, and culture—felt connected to one another in Christ. They shared their material resources with one another and eagerly received news and visits from members of distant churches.

Missionaries throughout the ages continued to follow in Paul's footsteps, carrying the good news of Jesus Christ around the globe. Because of their efforts, the Catholic Church is present on every continent today. Paul relied on the prayers of the Romans for protection and for the success of his ministry (Romans 15:30-32). Let us, too, pray for all those who preach the gospel, whether close to home or in foreign lands.

"Thank you, Father, that I have received so much love and support from brothers and sisters united to me in your universal church. Show me how I can actively help them, both with my prayers and with my talents and resources."

Romans 16:1-23

¹ I commend to you our sister Phoebe, a deaconess of the church at Cenchreae, ² that you may receive her in the Lord as befits the saints, and help her in whatever she may require from you, for she has been a helper of many and of myself as well.
³ Greet Prisca and Aquila, my fellow workers in Christ Jesus,
⁴ who risked their necks for my life, to whom not only I but also all the churches of the Gentiles give thanks; ⁵ greet also the church in their house. Greet my beloved Epaenetus, who was the first convert in Asia for Christ. ⁶ Greet Mary, who has worked hard among you.
⁷ Greet Andronicus and Junias, my kinsmen and my fellow prisoners; they are men of note among the apostles, and they were in Christ before me. ⁸ Greet Ampliatus, my beloved in the Lord. ⁹ Greet

Urbanus, our fellow worker in Christ, and my beloved Stachys. [10] Greet Apelles, who is approved in Christ. Greet those who belong to the family of Aristobulus. [11] Greet my kinsman Herodion. Greet those in the Lord who belong to the family of Narcissus. [12] Greet those workers in the Lord, Tryphaena and Tryphosa. Greet the beloved Persis, who has worked hard in the Lord. [13] Greet Rufus, eminent in the Lord, also his mother and mine. [14] Greet Asyncritus, Phlegon, Hermes, Patrobas, Hermas, and the brethren who are with them. [15] Greet Philologus, Julia, Nereus and his sister, and Olympas, and all the saints who are with them. [16] Greet one another with a holy kiss. All the churches of Christ greet you.

[17] I appeal to you, brethren, to take note of those who create dissensions and difficulties, in opposition to the doctrine which you have been taught; avoid them. [18] For such persons do not serve our Lord Christ, but their own appetites, and by fair and flattering words they deceive the hearts of the simple-minded. [19] For while your obedience is known to all, so that I rejoice over you, I would have you wise as to what is good and guileless as to what is evil; [20] then the God of peace will soon crush Satan under your feet. The grace of our Lord Jesus Christ be with you.

[21] Timothy, my fellow worker, greets you; so do Lucius and Jason and Sosipater, my kinsmen.

[22] I, Tertius, the writer of this letter, greet you in the Lord.

[23] Gaius, who is host to me and to the whole church, greets you. Erastus, the city treasurer, and our brother Quartus, greet you.

The last chapter of Romans contains a roster of names. More than twenty persons are greeted, most of whom are little known except through their relationship with the apostle Paul. For the most part, these gentile and Jewish Christian friends of Paul were from the lower strata of Roman society. Many of them apparently were slaves. Despite being little known, people like these were the bulwark of the early church because of their love and tireless service.

Phoebe (Romans 16:1), the bearer of the letter, was a deacon of the church at Cenchreae in Corinth. She taught women interested in Christianity, helped the poor, and had been a benefactor of Paul and many others. Whether her assistance was political, financial, or came under the label of hospitality, her service helped Paul's evangelistic efforts.

Prisca (also called Priscilla) and Aquila (Romans 16:3) are the most recognizable names. This Jewish Christian couple was expelled from Rome by the emperor Claudius and settled in Corinth. Like Paul, they worked as tentmakers, a common occupation that they used to honor God. Paul stayed with them on his first journey to Corinth (Acts 18:1-2), and they accompanied him to Ephesus. There they instructed many, including Apollos, a fervent preacher who "knew only the baptism of John" (18:24-26).

Prisca and Aquila taught Apollos about Jesus (Acts 18:26), and he became an effective evangelist. They "risked their necks" for Paul (Romans 16:4), possibly through their intervention on his behalf in a riot at Ephesus (Acts 19:23), and during his imprisonment there. One late tradition says that they were martyred for their faith at Rome.

Epaenetus (Romans 16:5) was the first Asian convert. Paul considered his conversion as the means through which the Roman province of Asia was consecrated to Christ.

Paul commended these little-known Christians for their selfless service, which was essential for the spread of the gospel and the building up of the body of Christ. Most of us are not called to be great and famous like Paul, Peter, or Apollos. We too may be virtually unknown, except to our congregations. Our calling lies in serving and evangelizing those with whom we come into contact each day. As we serve these people, we serve the Lord. All service (no matter how great or small) performed out of love for Christ bears witness to his love and power in our lives. Thus it builds and strengthens Christ's body on earth.

"Lord Jesus, you have called me, and I want to serve you. Use me to draw others to your abundant love."

Romans 16:25-27

25 Now to him who is able to strengthen you according to my gospel and the preaching of Jesus Christ, according to the revelation of the mystery which was kept secret for long ages 26 but is now disclosed and through the prophetic writings is made known to all nations, according to the command of the eternal God, to bring about the obedience of faith— 27 to the only wise God be glory for evermore through Jesus Christ! Amen.

Paul was not personally known by most of the people to whom he wrote this letter. Remember, he had yet to visit the city of Rome. However, during his missionary travels throughout Greece and Asia Minor, he had come to know many Christian brothers and sisters whom he counted as his friends and coworkers in the faith and, evidently, some of them had settled in Rome. Closing his letter with personal greetings to those there whom he knew and who knew him gave him good "references" for the whole church.

Among those Paul affectionately greeted by name were men and women from many different social backgrounds and different parts of the Roman Empire: wealthy patricians and middle-class tradesmen as well as slaves; Greeks, Latins, Jews, and people throughout Asia Minor. This list gives us a glimpse of the early Christians—people of all sorts—working together to make Jesus Christ and his gift of salvation known to their world.

Now Paul brings this letter to a close with a hymn of praise to the God who alone had enabled all of these people to stand firm and immovable as they lived out the gospel they had received. This prayer reminds us just how important it is that we too, like Paul's friends and fellow missionaries, proclaim the gospel to others. By sharing the good news with the people we encounter in our daily circumstances, we are making God's revelation known "to all nations, according to the command of the eternal God, to bring about the obedience of faith" (Romans 16:26).

Finally, notice how closely the end of this letter resembles its beginning. In Romans 16:25-27 we hear clear echoes of Paul's initial greeting to the Christians in Rome (1:2-6). By ending with a prayer that repeats what he said in his opening, Paul highlighted the theme that has run through his entire letter: God's plan for us is fulfilled in Jesus Christ. To him who has given us this great gift of salvation, "the only wise God be glory for evermore" (16:27). May our lives reflect this hymn of love, praise and gratitude!

"Thank you, Lord, for the many people who have shared their faith with me. Thank you for the witness they have been to me and for the strength I have gained from them. May many others come to know you and your gospel through my words and my life."

"Paul, Apostle of God"

GALATIANS
1:1–2:21

Galatians 1:1-5

1 Paul an apostle—not from men nor through man, but through Jesus Christ and God the Father, who raised him from the dead— 2 and all the brethren who are with me,

To the churches of Galatia:

3 Grace to you and peace from God the Father and our Lord Jesus Christ, 4 who gave himself for our sins to deliver us from the present evil age, according to the will of our God and Father; 5 to whom be the glory for ever and ever. Amen.

The news was unsettling. The church in Galatia—which Paul had personally founded—was showing signs of division and discord. Apparently, other missionaries had succeeded in convincing the Galatians that in addition to believing in Jesus they had to add observance of Jewish law, especially circumcision, for their salvation to be assured. Paul recognized that this was a significant distortion of the gospel and a danger to their faith. And so, he wrote them a passionate letter pleading with them to come back to the message he had first declared to them.

Paul wasted no time as he began his letter. He started by presenting his gospel in capsule form: God had raised Jesus from the dead (Galatians 1:1)—the same Jesus who "gave himself for our sins" (1:4)! This is the heart of the gospel message, and anything that spoke against the completeness of Jesus' sacrifice was off the mark.

Paul then went on to tell the Galatians that by his death, Jesus also "delivered us from the present evil age" (Galatians 1:4). In other words, he redeemed us not only from the sin that is within us, but from the sin that surrounds us as well. He has delivered us from a distorted worldview that is in conflict with God's love and mercy. He has delivered us from all the false values and philosophies that run counter to the truth of God. He has even delivered us from the forces of evil and sinful tendencies that want to play on our hearts and minds to ensnare us.

Just as the first-century Galatians were endangered by teachings that undermined their experience of freedom in Christ, we in the twenty-first century face similar threats. The philosophies of our "present evil age" tell us that God's love is conditional. This "age" tells us that forgiveness is hard to come by, and that we must also be reluctant to forgive. It tells us that Jesus' resurrection has no bearing on our lives, and that we shouldn't expect to have any "resurrection" experiences in our prayer or in our relationships with one another.

As you work through this powerful letter from St. Paul, ask the Holy Spirit to deepen your experience of Jesus. Ask him to show you the freedom Jesus has won for you. Trust that you too have been delivered from the philosophies of this world and that you can live as a new creation.

"Jesus, thank you for protecting me from the evil that is in the world. Help me to live in the full freedom you have won for me by your death and resurrection. By your Spirit, may I come to share this gospel of freedom with those around me."

Galatians 1:6-12

[6] I am astonished that you are so quickly deserting him who called you in the grace of Christ and turning to a different gospel— [7] not that there is another gospel, but there are some who trouble you and want to pervert the gospel of Christ. [8] But even if we, or an angel from heaven, should preach to you a gospel contrary to that which we preached to you, let him be accursed. [9] As we have said before, so now I say again, If any one is preaching to you a gospel contrary to that which you received, let him be accursed.

[10] Am I now seeking the favor of men, or of God? Or am I trying to please men? If I were still pleasing men, I should not be a servant of Christ.

[11] For I would have you know, brethren, that the gospel which was preached by me is not man's gospel. [12] For I did not receive it from man, nor was I taught it, but it came through a revelation of Jesus Christ.

Imagine the shock of parents receiving a telephone call from the police telling them that their child—whom they raised to obey God's commands—has been arrested for shoplifting. In a way, this astonishment at behavior that is completely unreasonable, destructive, and contrary to everything that has been taught, was in Paul's heart as he wrote to the Galatians. Later in his letter, he made the analogy himself: "My little children, with whom I am again in travail until Christ be formed in you! I could wish to be present with you now and to change my tone, for I am perplexed about you" (Galatians 4:19-20).

What was the behavior that produced such a strong reaction in Paul? It was that even in the face of the Galatians' experience of the love of God and the freedom they had received through the death and resurrection of Jesus, they were forsaking the gospel that had brought them this freedom, and were turning to "a different gospel" (Galatians 1:6). Rather than trusting what God had done for them in Christ, they were looking to the rules and regulations of the Jewish law as their justification before God.

Unfortunately, it is possible for us today to fall victim to the same temptation, and many do. Even good things such as faithfulness to religious duties, being considerate of others, and serving the needy—all important parts of our Christian lives—can never supplant faith in Jesus and the knowledge of what he has done for us. Rather, they must flow from it.

It is important to ask ourselves: "Do I know that through my baptism into Jesus and faith in him I am set free from sin? Have I experienced the power of the gospel to save me and set me free? Is the good news I believe centered on Jesus and his cross and resurrection? Is it empowered by the Holy Spirit? If I were approached with 'another gospel,' would everything I know about God, along with my experience of his power in my life, prevent me from forsaking the truth of Jesus Christ?"

"Lord Jesus, you want the gospel to come to us in demonstration of power leading to freedom and salvation. Heal anything in me that would hinder this work of your power, and raise my expectations of what you want to do in my life and in the life of the whole church."

Galatians 1:13-24

13 For you have heard of my former life in Judaism, how I persecuted the church of God violently and tried to destroy it; 14 and I advanced in Judaism beyond many of my own age among my people, so extremely zealous was I for the traditions of my fathers. 15 But when he who had set me apart before I was born, and had called me through his grace, 16 was pleased to reveal his Son to me, in order that I might preach him among the Gentiles, I did not confer with flesh and blood, 17 nor did I go up to Jerusalem to those who were apostles before me, but I went away into Arabia; and again I returned to Damascus.

18 Then after three years I went up to Jerusalem to visit Cephas, and remained with him fifteen days. 19 But I saw none of the other apostles except James the Lord's brother. 20 (In what I am writing to you, before God, I do not lie!) 21 Then I went into the regions of Syria and Cili'cia. 22 And I was still not known by sight to the churches of Christ in Judea; 22 they only heard it said, "He who once persecuted us is now preaching the faith he once tried to destroy." 24 And they glorified God because of me. ✍

The apostle Paul was able to state the gospel with such boldness and clarity because he himself had a powerful encounter with the Lord Jesus. Paul received the gospel directly from Jesus in a revelation that shook him to the core (Galatians 1:12; Acts 9:1-9). And, as a result of this experience, Paul's life took a radically different direction than the one he had mapped out for himself. He knew that God had called him to preach the gospel to the Gentiles, and his encounter with Jesus on the road to Damascus impelled him to devote the rest of his life to fulfilling his call.

Paul's emphasis on his experience of Jesus raises for us the question of our experience. Have you encountered Jesus Christ? Do you know him personally? Have you experienced the power of his grace and forgiveness? Of course Paul's experience was extraordinary—even unique. Nevertheless, Jesus wants to give each of us a personal knowledge of himself and of his power in us. He wants each of us to receive a revelation of him that pierces our hearts and transforms our lives.

Every day, Jesus is eager to reveal himself to us more deeply—in our work, with our families, and in a special way at Mass. Every day, he is eager to call us to a particular share in the mission of spreading the good news of Jesus Christ to others. It is our personal encounters with the Lord Jesus that will transform our lives and empower us to fulfill our callings in the world.

No matter what kind of experience we have had of Jesus up to now, he invites us to a deeper and more powerful revelation of him and his grace. We are all called to a life of holiness; we can all be empowered to bear abundant fruit in our missions. Are you open to a closer encounter with the Lord? Ask God for more. Seek him, and he will reveal himself to you more deeply. He will give you new power to lead the life and accomplish the mission he has entrusted to you.

"Lord Jesus, thank you for revealing yourself to me. I love you, Lord, and I want to know you better. Holy Spirit, thank you for your promise to transform me, so that I might live in closer union with Jesus and share the gospel more effectively."

Galatians 2:1-14

[1] Then after fourteen years I went up again to Jerusalem with Barnabas, taking Titus along with me. [2] I went up by revelation; and I laid before them (but privately before those who were of repute) the gospel which I preach among the Gentiles, lest somehow I should be running or had run in vain. [3] But even Titus, who was with me, was not compelled to be circumcised, though he was a Greek. [4] But because of false brethren secretly brought in, who slipped in to spy out our freedom which we have in Christ Jesus, that they might bring us into bondage— [5] to them we did not yield submission even for a moment, that the truth of the gospel might be preserved for you. [6] And from those who were reputed to be something (what they were makes no difference to me; God shows no partiality)—those, I say, who were of repute added nothing to me; [7] but on the contrary, when they saw that I had been entrusted with the gospel to the uncircumcised, just as Peter had been entrusted with the gospel to the circumcised [8] (for he who worked through Peter for the mission to the circumcised worked through me also for the Gentiles), [9] and when they perceived the grace that was given to me, James and Cephas and John, who were reputed to be pillars, gave to me and Barnabas the right hand of fellowship, that we should go to the Gentiles and they to the circumcised; [10] only they would have us remember the poor, which very thing I was eager to do. [11] But when Cephas came to Antioch I opposed him to his face, because he stood condemned. [12] For before certain men came from James, he ate with the Gentiles; but when they came he drew back and separated himself, fearing the circumcision party. [13] And with him the rest of the Jews acted insincerely, so that even Barnabas was carried away by their insincerity. [14] But when I saw that they were

not straightforward about the truth of the gospel, I said to Cephas before them all, "If you, though a Jew, live like a Gentile and not like a Jew, how can you compel the Gentiles to live like Jews?" ✒

The famous confrontation between Peter and Paul has puzzled many New Testament readers who find it difficult to understand how two apostles could have been at odds with one another. A closer look reveals that Paul's public challenge of Peter was motivated by desire to protect and promote the "truth of the gospel" (Galatians 2:14), and not by any competitive self-interest.

Peter, the head of the apostles, had come to stay for a time with the believers at Antioch. While there he enjoyed full social fellowship with the gentile converts to Christianity. This had been his practice ever since the Spirit revealed to him that he was free to eat the food of Gentiles, even though—as a Jew—he had always considered certain foods unclean (Acts 10:28).

But when some Jewish Christians from Jerusalem visited Antioch, Peter withdrew from the Gentiles so as not to offend the visitors' sensibilities. To many, Peter's behavior probably seemed quite reasonable—or at least politically expedient—given the circumstances. Many of the other Jews, including Paul's close companion, Barnabas, readily followed his lead. In reality, Peter was being insincere, acting out of fear rather than out of humble obedience to God.

Paul's insight into the consequences of this concession compelled him to challenge Peter—the rock of the church—in a public setting. Paul understood that by refusing to eat with the uncircumcised, Peter was sending a signal that something was lacking in their faith—that they were somehow second-class Christians who could be improved by adherence to Jewish law. What Peter had done was an offense against the truth of the gospel. In effect, he implied that the redemption wrought by Christ's death on the cross was not enough to justify a person before God; observance of the Mosaic Law had to be included. Paul saw the error of this line of thinking, and had to risk sounding disrespectful in order to protect the Antioch believers' faith—and ours.

Let us be grateful that as a result of the first apostles' struggles in understanding the faith, we now have the gospel clearly spelled out for us, both in Scripture and in the Spirit-inspired tradition of the church. Let us also seek to uphold the truth of the gospel in our lives, even if it means taking risks. Surely the Lord is worthy.

Galatians 2:15-21

[15] We ourselves, who are Jews by birth and not Gentile sinners,
[16] yet who know that a man is not justified by works of the law but through faith in Jesus Christ, even we have believed in Christ Jesus, in order to be justified by faith in Christ, and not by works of the law, because by works of the law shall no one be justified. [17] But if, in our endeavor to be justified in Christ, we ourselves were found to be sinners, is Christ then an agent of sin? Certainly not! [18] But if I build up again those things which I tore down, then I prove myself a transgressor. [19] For I through the law died to the law, that I might live to God. [20] I have been crucified with Christ; it is no longer I who live, but Christ who lives in me; and the life I now live in the flesh I live by faith in the Son of God, who loved me and gave himself for me. [21] I do not nullify the grace of God; for if justification were through the law, then Christ died to no purpose.

I have been crucified with Christ; it is no longer I who live,
but Christ who lives in me. (Galatians 2:20)

These words resound in our ears like a shout of triumph and fill our hearts with a sense of hope and confidence. But these words are also mysterious, and their full meaning can elude us. What does it mean to be "crucified with Christ"? Surely not that we have been physically nailed to a cross just as Jesus was. The answer lies in understanding what happens to us when we are baptized.

St. John Chrysostom, one of the early Fathers of the Church, explained Paul's logic in this way: "In these words, 'I am crucified with Christ,' Paul alludes to baptism. . . . For as by death he signifies not what is commonly understood, but a death to sin; so by life, he signifies a deliverance from sin. For a man cannot live to God other than by dying to sin."

So we do "die" at baptism, but it is a spiritual death—a death to sin. On the one hand, this might seem like a vague and theoretical kind of death, or not even a death at all. But in reality, it is the deepest and most important aspect of our lives. Who we are as spiritual people is far more important—both to God and to us—than who we are as physical people. The fact that one of us has blond hair and another has brown hair is surely secondary to the question of whether or not our lives are open to the power and love of Christ. So too is the question of whether we are nine years old or ninety-nine years old. It is the spiritual aspects of who we are that have the greatest influence over the way we live in the world.

We are so accustomed to living on the physical level. But Jesus came and died so that we might live a new life—a life that is in direct contact with the Creator of heaven and earth. At the heart of Paul's words is the recognition that without the death of baptism, without being united with Jesus' death on the cross, there would be no openness to Christ. There would be no hope of everlasting life. There would be no way to overcome the sin that keeps us bound to this world.

The death we experience through baptism breaks the power of sin. Then, just as Christ was raised from the dead, we also are raised to newness of life—to a new life that is nothing less than the risen Christ living in us. May we all find the faith and the freedom to echo Paul's words!

A Devotional Commentary on Romans and Galatians

The Blessing of Abraham Given to Gentiles

GALATIANS
3:1-29

Galatians 3:1-5

¹ O foolish Galatians! Who has bewitched you, before whose eyes Jesus Christ was publicly portrayed as crucified? ² Let me ask you only this: Did you receive the Spirit by works of the law, or by hearing with faith? ³ Are you so foolish? Having begun with the Spirit, are you now ending with the flesh? ⁴ Did you experience so many things in vain?—if it really is in vain. ⁵ Does he who supplies the Spirit to you and works miracles among you do so by works of the law, or by hearing with faith?

Just after Jesus had risen from the dead, he appeared to two disciples as they were walking to Emmaus (Luke 24:13-35). When they sat down to dinner, Jesus blessed and broke the bread, and "their eyes were opened and they recognized him"(24:30-31). Many of us would love to have an experience like these two privileged disciples.

The Galatians, on the other hand, were probably not present in Jerusalem to witness Jesus' crucifixion or to see the risen Lord with their own eyes. How, then, could Paul address them as people "before whose eyes Jesus Christ was publicly portrayed as crucified" (Galatians 3:1)? Wasn't he being too severe with this second generation of disciples?

The reality is that the Galatians had received a revelation of Jesus just as powerful as the two disciples on the road to Emmaus. In both instances it was the Holy Spirit who opened the eyes of their hearts to see the Lord and cause the word of God to burn in their hearts (Luke 24:32; Galatians 3:5). The Galatians were not just a group of "regular" men and women. Like the first disciples, their lives had been touched and transformed as the Spirit revealed the love of Christ to their hearts. Now, however, their vision had been clouded; their trust in the Lord's love had diminished.

Many of us know what it is like to have our vision of God's love clouded. It can be so easy for our focus to shift from the Lord to ourselves. This is why we have the precious gift of prayer. At any moment we can turn our hearts to God and allow his Spirit to touch and fill us with his love. Through prayer, our vision can be restored, and we can once more "see" Jesus Christ, crucified for our sins and raised to life for our salvation.

Speaking on prayer at a youth rally in New Orleans in 1987, Pope John Paul II said:

Prayer . . . turns your attention away from yourself and directs your mind and your heart toward the Lord. If we look at ourselves, with our own limitations and sins, we quickly give way to sadness and discouragement. If we keep our eyes on the Lord, then our hearts are filled with hope, our minds washed in the light of truth, and we come to know the fullness of the Gospel with all its promise and life.

May we too fix our eyes on Jesus and allow his Spirit to open our hearts.

Galatians 3:6-14

6   Thus Abraham "believed God, and it was reckoned to him as righteousness." 7 So you see that it is men of faith who are the sons of Abraham. 8 And the scripture, foreseeing that God would justify the Gentiles by faith, preached the gospel beforehand to Abraham, saying, "In you shall all the nations be blessed." 9 So then, those who are men of faith are blessed with Abraham who had faith.
10   For all who rely on works of the law are under a curse; for it is written, "Cursed be every one who does not abide by all things written in the book of the law, and do them." 11 Now it is evident that no man is justified before God by the law; for "He who through faith is righteous shall live"; 12 but the law does not rest on faith, for "He who does them shall live by them." 13 Christ redeemed us from the curse of the law, having become a curse for us—for it is written, "Cursed be every one who hangs on a tree"— 14 that in Christ Jesus the blessing of Abraham might come upon the Gentiles, that we might receive the promise of the Spirit through faith. ✍

Paul tried to get the Galatians to see that if a person has faith in Jesus, there is no need to undertake the observance of the Mosaic Law. To demonstrate this truth, he pointed to the great model of faith—Abraham. God called Abraham to uproot himself from his country, and Abraham responded, because he trusted God. God's promises of children and land must have seemed rather distant to him, yet Abraham continued to follow him, waiting years until he saw the promises fulfilled. In faith, Abraham surrendered everything to God, even his son Isaac, because he had experienced God's touch, and that touch had set his heart on fire.

Abraham's unshakable trust pleased God. Abraham "believed the LORD; and he reckoned it to him as righteousness" (Genesis 15:6). It was Abraham's belief in God's love that moved him to such radical obedience; this in turn led to abundant blessings. That is why Paul applied the words of the prophet Habakkuk to Abraham: "The righteous shall live by his faith" (Habakkuk 2:4).

When people asked Jesus, "What must we do, to be doing the works of God?" Jesus answered, "Believe in him whom he has sent. . . I am the living bread which came down from heaven; if any one eats of this bread, he will live forever" (John 6:28-29,51). The way to everlasting life is to believe in Jesus who gave his body and blood at Calvary. In receiving him we have forgiveness of sins and new life welling up into eternity.

Do you believe that God loves you so much that he chose to rescue you "by his grace as a gift, through the redemption which is in Christ Jesus" (Romans 3:24)? Through Jesus, God not only acquits us of guilt; he transforms us within. Can you trust that "justification is not only the remission of sins but also the sanctification and renewal of the interior man" (*Catechism of the Catholic Church*, 1989)? These truths are central to being a true follower of Christ. Let us obey God, not in an effort to gain his favor, but in response to his saving love.

"Jesus, thank you for revealing yourself to me. I love you because you were so humble as to sacrifice your life—even for me. Lord, I put my faith in you."

Galatians 3:15-21

15   To give a human example, brethren: no one annuls even a man's will, or adds to it, once it has been ratified. 16 Now the promises were made to Abraham and to his offspring. It does not say, "And to offsprings," referring to many; but, referring to one, "And to your offspring," which is Christ. 17 This is what I mean: the law, which came four hundred and thirty years afterward, does not annul a covenant previously ratified by God, so as to make the promise void. 18 For if the inheritance is by the law, it is no longer by promise; but God gave it to Abraham by a promise.
19   Why then the law? It was added because of transgressions, till the offspring should come to whom the promise had been made; and it was ordained by angels through an intermediary. 20 Now an intermediary implies more than one; but God is one.
21   Is the law then against the promises of God? Certainly not; for if a law had been given which could make alive, then righteousness would indeed be by the law.

God had promised a great inheritance to Abraham: his own land, descendants as numerous as the stars in the sky, and an intimate relationship with the Lord of the heavens. And what's even greater is that Abraham didn't have to earn these blessings; God gave them to him by grace—freely and undeservedly. All Abraham had to do was to believe God when he spoke (Galatians 3:6). Paul stressed this point in his reasoning with the Galatians because he wanted them to break out of thinking that they had to earn God's favor, life, and love.

When God made the covenant with Abraham, he ratified it only with love (Genesis 15:1-6). There were no conditions, no strings attached, no sacrifices required—it was just love flowing from his desire to give himself to his creation.

This is God's primary interest, that we know him as one who loves us. At the very beginning, God revealed himself not as a law-giver demanding obedience, but as a Father offering blessing and protection. The law came 430 years later (Galatians 3:17). He showed himself not as a taskmaster concerned chiefly with works, but as a lover delighting in his beloved.

Paul chided the Galatians, who had lost this vision of God and were beginning to substitute it with a sense of working to please God. This is why the story of Abraham was so important for Paul. Before Abraham did anything, while he was still a pagan, God revealed his love to him.

Obeying rules and regulations, working harder, reading more holy books are not how we come to know God's love for us. All these things are good things, but in and of themselves they won't open us up to God's Holy Spirit in the measure he wants to pour it out. Consider how he revealed himself to Abraham: graciously, requiring nothing.

We risk missing all the blessings God has for us if we rely solely on our efforts to know God and to please him. Remember, "God shows his love for us in that while we were yet sinners Christ died for us" (Romans 5:8). Like Abraham, we didn't do anything to earn it. We have only to believe it, as incredible as that seems!

"Faithful Father, thank you for your love. I don't deserve it. I can't earn it. But I desperately need to know it. Let your love flow over me today. Open my eyes to see it and my heart to receive it."

Galatians 3:22-29

[22] But the scripture consigned all things to sin, that what was promised to faith in Jesus Christ might be given to those who believe.
[23] Now before faith came, we were confined under the law, kept under restraint until faith should be revealed. [24] So that the law was our custodian until Christ came, that we might be justified by faith. [25] But now that faith has come, we are no longer under a custodian; [26] for in Christ Jesus you are all sons of God, through faith. [27] For as many of you as were baptized into Christ have put on Christ. [28] There is neither Jew nor Greek, there is neither slave nor free, there is neither male nor female; for you are all one in Christ Jesus. [29] And if you are Christ's, then you are Abraham's offspring, heirs according to promise.

St. Paul saw the arrival of Christ as marking the end of one age—the age of law—and the beginning of a new one—the age of Christ. For him, the Law of Moses was like the household slave who in ancient times was assigned to supervise each child until they reached maturity. Likewise, the law was meant to discipline us by pointing out sin and helping keep our behavior in check.

Ultimately, however, the law was meant to show us not only our outward behavior, but also the state of our hearts. Its ultimate goal was to reveal to us the power of sin dwelling in our hearts and our inability to free ourselves from sin's grasp. The true grace of the law is to move us to cry out to God for the mercy and freedom that only he can give. Seen in this light, the law is the first gift that opens us up to all the gifts that God wants to shower on us in Christ.

Now that sin has been defeated and the Holy Spirit poured out, God's law can be written on our hearts. What was once a guide to outward behavior has become a living principle of life. As we lay aside the old clothing of living solely by outward commands and put on Christ's new robe of righteousness, we grow up spiritually and assume the privileges and responsibilities of mature sons and daughters.

God doesn't want us relating to him and each other in ways that are guided solely by rules. He wants loving responses that come to us naturally. He wants us to think and feel the same as he does. He wants us to obey him because we love him. As we allow the Holy Spirit to write the laws on our hearts, we will come to see that there are no distinctions among God's children. We are all debtors to God's grace and desperately in need of Christ. Let us embrace each other not only as coheirs in God's kingdom, but also as codebtors in need of God's grace.

"Jesus, that you would humble yourself to live in my heart fills me with gratitude. I praise you for sending me your Spirit to transform me into your very image."

Children of God through Faith

GALATIANS
4:1–5:1

Galatians 4:1-7

[1] I mean that the heir, as long as he is a child, is no better than a slave, though he is the owner of all the estate; [2] but he is under guardians and trustees until the date set by the father. [3] So with us; when we were children, we were slaves to the elemental spirits of the universe. [4] But when the time had fully come, God sent forth his Son, born of woman, born under the law, [5] to redeem those who were under the law, so that we might receive adoption as sons. [6] And because you are sons, God has sent the Spirit of his Son into our hearts, crying, "Abba! Father!" [7] So through God you are no longer a slave but a son, and if a son then an heir. ⌁

God sent his Son, born of a woman. . . so that we might receive adoption as sons. (Galatians 4:4-5)

Just as the Son of God was born of a woman—a pure and humble virgin—so too all the adopted children of God are born of a virginal bride; the spotless bride of Christ which is the church. Throughout the centuries, saints and church leaders have commented on the symbolic role that Mary, the Mother of God, plays in our understanding of the church and, indeed the real role she played in the Father's plan of salvation.

At the birth of her first child, the first person born under the reign of sin, Eve said: "I have produced a man with the help of the Lord" (Genesis 4:1). These words apply in a unique way to Mary as well, the one who would bear the firstborn of the new creation, for with the help of the Lord she too brought forth a son. In this way, Mary truly is the

Mother of God, for Jesus—fully God and fully man—took form within her womb and was born of her.

Mary's title, "Mother of God," carries with it the related title, "Mother of the Church," a title she received at the foot of her son's cross. In John's account of the crucifixion, Jesus' last act was to establish a mother-son relationship between Mary and his beloved disciple. "And from that hour the disciple took her into his own home" (John 19:27). In a new way, Mary had "with the help of the Lord . . . brought forth a man," the firstborn of many brothers and sisters, the head of a new race.

As the new Eve giving birth to a new humanity in Christ, Mary became the mother of the church, the gathering of all those disciples who are loved by God and who love him in return. She whose soul was pierced as she witnessed her son's agony (Luke 2:35), suffered the pain of giving birth to sons and daughters of God. It cost Mary not only her son, but every attachment to the ways of the world in order for her to bear fruit for God.

Let us echo Mary's prayer as Jesus' mother and as the mother of the whole church: "Here am I, the servant of the Lord; let it be with me according to your word" (Luke 1:38).

Galatians 4:8-20

[8] Formerly, when you did not know God, you were in bondage to beings that by nature are no gods; [9] but now that you have come to know God, or rather to be known by God, how can you turn back again to the weak and beggarly elemental spirits, whose slaves you want to be once more? [10] You observe days, and months, and seasons, and years!

¹¹ I am afraid I have labored over you in vain.

¹²   Brethren, I beseech you, become as I am, for I also have become as you are. You did me no wrong; ¹³ you know it was because of a bodily ailment that I preached the gospel to you at first; ¹⁴ and though my condition was a trial to you, you did not scorn or despise me, but received me as an angel of God, as Christ Jesus. ¹⁵ What has become of the satisfaction you felt? For I bear you witness that, if possible, you would have plucked out your eyes and given them to me. ¹⁶ Have I then become your enemy by telling you the truth?

¹⁷ They make much of you, but for no good purpose; they want to shut you out, that you may make much of them. ¹⁸ For a good purpose it is always good to be made much of, and not only when I am present with you. ¹⁹ My little children, with whom I am again in travail until Christ be formed in you! ²⁰ I could wish to be present with you now and to change my tone, for I am perplexed about you.

My little children, with whom I am again in travail
until Christ be formed in you! (Galatians 4:19)

Paul loved the Galatians deeply. Like a shepherd, he wanted to guide them, guard them from predators, and bind their wounds. And, like Jesus the Good Shepherd, Paul's heart burned with concern for the church, which was beginning to grow as the gospel spread. Reading through this passionate letter to the Galatians, it becomes clear that Paul did not come by this pastoral heart solely by virtue of his own natural compassion. God had revealed himself, and his vast love, to Paul in the person of Jesus, and that revelation transformed his life (Galatians 1:11-15).

Formerly, Paul had burned with zeal for the Jewish law and the traditions of his fathers (Galatians 1:14). At that time, perhaps, it had enraged Paul that Jesus' followers didn't live by the strict requirements of the law (1:13). But after Jesus had touched his heart and opened his eyes (Acts 9:1-19), Paul understood how concern for rules, zeal for human tradition, and reliance on human efforts can only enslave and, ultimately, choke off spiritual life. Paul wanted the Galatians to share in the same life which God had poured out on him—a life freed from sin and judgment, a life freed from enslavement to the law.

Paul didn't have an easy time of it. To strengthen and encourage communities of believers like the Galatians, he endured hostility, beatings, imprisonment, and deliberate attempts to undermine the gospel he preached. Though only a few today experience the violent opposition Paul did, still our bishops and pastors have no easy time shepherding their flocks. Yet God is the same. He continues to call men and women to care for his people. He is always ready to pour out his love in the hearts of pastors.

Brothers and sisters, do we pray for all who lead us in faith? Do we pray that God will comfort and strengthen them? Their task is monumental. Let's pray that God will give them the wisdom and fortitude they need to point out the way of peace and freedom in Jesus. Let's pray, especially, that God will fill their hearts to overflowing with his tender love, just as he did for Paul.

"Father, bless those whom you have called to shepherd your flock. Gather them in your arms and comfort them. Renew their desire to serve you. Holy Spirit, guide all pastors according to your wisdom. Give them an increase of the Father's love, so that they will overflow with that same love for those in their care."

Galatians 4: 21–5:1

21 Tell me, you who desire to be under law, do you not hear the law?

22 For it is written that Abraham had two sons, one by a slave and one by a free woman. 23 But the son of the slave was born according to the flesh, the son of the free woman through promise. 24 Now this is an allegory: these women are two covenants. One is from Mount Sinai, bearing children for slavery; she is Hagar. 25 Now Hagar is Mount Sinai in Arabia; she corresponds to the present Jerusalem, for she is in slavery with her children. 26 But the Jerusalem above is free, and she is our mother. 27 For it is written,

"Rejoice, O barren one who does not bear;

break forth and shout, you who are not in travail;

for the children of the desolate one are many more

than the children of her that is married."

28 Now we, brethren, like Isaac, are children of promise. 29 But as at that time he who was born according to the flesh persecuted him who was born according to the Spirit, so it is now. 30 But what does the scripture say? "Cast out the slave and her son; for the son of the slave shall not inherit with the son of the free woman." 31 So, brethren, we are not children of the slave but of the free woman. 1 For freedom Christ has set us free; stand fast therefore, and do not submit again to a yoke of slavery. ☙

Paul exhorted the Galatians, "Become as I am!" not out of arrogance or conceit, but because he knew the privilege of being a child of God (Galatians 4:12). He knew the freedom of being under the care and guidance of the Holy Spirit. He had also known servitude as a child of the law, born to a life regulated by proscription and obligation to all its dictates—born "for slavery" (4:24).

Under the old covenant (represented by Hagar), God provided a guardian and guide for his people—the law—to direct them until the coming of Christ (Galatians 3:24). Those born under the law were bound to lifelong, unremitting service to it. Nevertheless, the law was part of God's plan to form a people and to prepare them for the new and everlasting covenant that Jesus instituted when the time had fully come (4:4). Just as children need guidance, God's people needed direction until the coming of Christ. Paul did not argue against the law. He taught that the law was part of God's plan, but that numerous requirements (circumcision, dietary restrictions, etc.) were no longer binding under the new covenant in Jesus' blood. Through faith in Christ, God's people would become children of the promise given to Abraham (Genesis 17:19-21). They would become the free children of Sarah.

Now that Christ has come, we can all become children of the Father. The "Judaizers" wanted to subject Christianity to the law. But to adopt once more the practices of the Jewish law as a means of salvation would be to forfeit freedom in Christ. Christ has exonerated us from our sins against God, freeing us from their penalty and the claims and accusations of the evil one. Christ won our freedom on the cross; nothing else is required. Jesus did all that was necessary. We have only to confess our sins, believe in him, and be baptized. (Acts 2:38). We are free to approach God, free to live a life of faith in Jesus. We are now temples of the Spirit, who empowers us to live in accord with the commandments Christ.

"Father, we thank you for never leaving your people without guidance. We thank you, too, for the freedom we have received because your Son died on the cross. Help us stand firm in faith, unmoved by any argument that would lead us back to slavery. Fill our hearts with your love so, that we might love you in return."

Called to Freedom

GALATIANS
5:2–6:18

Galatians 5:2-6

2 Now I, Paul, say to you that if you receive circumcision, Christ will be of no advantage to you. 3 I testify again to every man who receives circumcision that he is bound to keep the whole law. 4 You are severed from Christ, you who would be justified by the law; you have fallen away from grace. 5 For through the Spirit, by faith, we wait for the hope of righteousness. 6 For in Christ Jesus neither circumcision nor uncircumcision is of any avail, but faith working through love.

Paul's distress over the state of the Galatians is evident in these impassioned words. However, while Paul had become exasperated with the Galatians, he did not walk away from them. Instead, he explained to them the truths of the gospel all over again, emphasizing the free gift of salvation they had received in Christ. Though the Galatians were straying, Paul was confident that they could still return to the truth. The "hope of righteousness" through "the Spirit, by faith" (Galatians 5:5) kept Paul optimistic.

Repentance and restoration through the blood of Jesus was a possibility for the Galatians, just as it is for us when we wander. Paul did not give up on them because he knew that the Lord never gives up on us. Do you feel that you have wandered from Jesus? Do you feel distant from the comforting and reassuring voice of the Spirit? Don't give up! God is always waiting, always ready, to receive you back. Remember the familiar saying that, even if you walk one hundred miles away from God, it only takes one step to return to him.

C. S. Lewis, the popular Christian thinker, once wrote:

A Christian is not a man who never goes wrong, but a man who is enabled to repent and pick himself up and begin over again after each stumble—because the Christ-life is inside him, repairing him all the time, enabling him to repeat (in some degree) the kind of voluntary death which Christ Himself carried out.

That is why the Christian is in a different position from other people who are trying to be good. They hope, by being good, to please God. . . . But the Christian thinks any good he does comes from the Christ-life inside him. He does not think God will love us because we are good, but that God will make us good because he loves us; just as the roof of a greenhouse does not attract the sun because it is bright, but becomes bright because the sun shines on it. (*Mere Christianity*, Chapter 5)

"Lord Jesus, by your death and resurrection, you have set me free. Thank you for your constant faithfulness, even when I sin against you. Help me to recognize my failings and give me the grace of repentance. I am ever grateful for your boundless mercy."

Galatians 5:7-15

[7] You were running well; who hindered you from obeying the truth?
[8] This persuasion is not from him who calls you. [9] A little leaven
leavens the whole lump. [10] I have confidence in the Lord that you
will take no other view than mine; and he who is troubling you will
bear his judgment, whoever he is. [11] But if I, brethren, still preach
circumcision, why am I still persecuted? In that case the stumbling
block of the cross has been removed. [12] I wish those who unsettle
you would mutilate themselves!
[13] For you were called to freedom, brethren; only do not use your
freedom as an opportunity for the flesh, but through love be servants of
one another. [14] For the whole law is fulfilled in one word, "You shall
love your neighbor as yourself." [15] But if you bite and devour one
another take heed that you are not consumed by one another.

You were called to freedom. (Galatians 5:13)

The Galatians were on the right track, "running well," as Paul
said (Galatians 5:7). They relied on faith in Christ, not legal
observance of rules or their own efforts, for their sense of righteousness. They believed that Jesus' death on the cross cancelled their
sin and made them acceptable to God. And it was through faith in that
act alone that they experienced peace and hope from the Holy Spirit.
But then someone—or a group of people—introduced a little "yeast"
(5:9) and succeeded in unsettling their faith. The Galatians began to
waver: Maybe circumcision was necessary after all; perhaps observing
the Jewish law was necessary for them to know salvation.

"No!" Paul thundered. "You were called to freedom" (Galatians 5:13).

And the entire New Testament thunders along with him. We were called to freedom from circumcision (5:2); freedom from earning titles and positions of honor (Matthew 20:26); freedom from ever trying to earn salvation through works (Ephesians 2:9); freedom from regulations about dress, eating and fasting, tithing and washing (Colossians 2:16-22). None of these had the power to make us right before God.

Jesus really has called us to freedom! Freedom from the guilt and shame of sin (Revelation 1:5), and freedom from slavery to sin (Romans 7:6). In Christ, we are free to work, to serve God joyfully and eagerly (Hebrews 9:14). We are free to love others, even those whom we find it hard to love. In fact, we are called to freedom for the very purpose that, through love, we can be servants of one another (Galatians 5:13). Not only is this possible; it's our calling!

The world tells us that freedom is the right to think and say and do whatever we want. But Jesus says that freedom means release from anything that prevents us from thinking and saying and doing what God wants. The more we know what Jesus has done for us, the more our faith is grounded on what he has accomplished in his death and resurrection, the more we're free to be vessels for the Holy Spirit—freed from preoccupation with sin, with "how I'm doing," and with following rules. Then, unhindered from obeying the truth, we begin to fulfill the greatest of all commands: "You shall love your neighbor as yourself" (Galatians 5:13-14).

In faith and trust, in hope and joy, let's all embrace our freedom today. We have been called to a radical freedom. Let's manifest this freedom to the whole world!

"Jesus, I rejoice in your death, for on that cross, you set me free. All praise to you, blessed Redeemer, for freeing me from guilt and shame and the shackles of sin! Thank you that I can love and serve you, and not merely myself, today."

Galatians 5: 16-26

[16] But I say, walk by the Spirit, and do not gratify the desires of the flesh. [17] For the desires of the flesh are against the Spirit, and the desires of the Spirit are against the flesh; for these are opposed to each other, to prevent you from doing what you would. [18] But if you are led by the Spirit you are not under the law. [19] Now the works of the flesh are plain: fornication, impurity, licentiousness, [20] idolatry, sorcery, enmity, strife, jealousy, anger, selfishness, dissension, party spirit, [21] envy, drunkenness, carousing, and the like. I warn you, as I warned you before, that those who do such things shall not inherit the kingdom of God.[22] But the fruit of the Spirit is love, joy, peace, patience, kindness, goodness, faithfulness, [23] gentleness, self-control; against such there is no law. [24] And those who belong to Christ Jesus have crucified the flesh with its passions and desires.
[25] If we live by the Spirit, let us also walk by the Spirit. [26] Let us have no self-conceit, no provoking of one another, no envy of one another.

W hat Christian doesn't want to experience the fruit of the Spirit in his life (Galatians 5:22-23)? But isn't our experience of life more often like what Paul described as the works of the flesh (5:19-21)? Examine a typical day. Does your life reflect more the works of the flesh or the fruit of the Spirit? As Christians, we should be growing in our experience of the fruit of the Spirit. How is this to occur in our lives?

Paul contrasted the works of the flesh with the fruit of the Spirit. The difference between "work" and "fruit" is important to understand. The flesh is by nature hostile to God (Romans 8:7) and itself does the works. From within us come these evil undertakings. The fruit of the Spirit, however, is a result of the work of God in us. Good fruit is not the result of our own will power but is a product of our cooperation with God in us.

If our flesh does its "works" naturally and is opposed to the Spirit, how then can we live by the Spirit and not according to the flesh? Paul answered this way: "Those who belong to Christ Jesus have crucified the flesh with its passions and desires" (Galatians 5:24). If we believe that Jesus is the Son of God who was crucified for our sins, then we know that our flesh has been dealt with by the power of the cross.

As we see these works of the flesh in our lives, we can turn to the cross of Christ and pray: "Jesus, I know that you died for me and because you died, I no longer have to live this way. I call on the power of your cross to crucify my flesh right now, so that I may live according to the Spirit, and not by the demands of my flesh." As we do this, we shall see victory over the flesh as part of our daily experience.

The marvelous thing is that it does not just stop there! We can go on to experience the fruit of the Spirit. We can continue to pray: "Holy Spirit, come and move me today to bear the fruit that only you can produce in me. I want to cooperate with you. I believe that by the power of the cross my flesh is crucified, and that by the power of the Spirit I can lead a new life."

Galatians 6:1-10

1   Brethren, if a man is overtaken in any trespass, you who are spiritual should restore him in a spirit of gentleness. Look to yourself, lest you too be tempted. 2 Bear one another's burdens, and so fulfil the law of Christ. 3 For if any one thinks he is something, when he is nothing, he deceives himself. 4 But let each one test his own work, and then his reason to boast will be in himself alone and not in his neighbor. 5 For each man will have to bear his own load.
6   Let him who is taught the word share all good things with him who teaches.
7   Do not be deceived; God is not mocked, for whatever a man sows, that he will also reap. 8 For he who sows to his own flesh will from the flesh reap corrution; but he who sows to the Spirit will from the Spirit reap eternal life 9 And let us not grow weary in well-doing, for in due season we shall reap, if we do not lose heart. 10 So then, as we have opportunity, let us do good to all men, and especially to those who are of the household of faith.

Bear one another's burdens, and so fulfill the law of Christ.
(Galatians 6:2)

On the night before he died, Jesus gave his disciples a "new commandment" to love one another even as he himself had loved them. Then he stressed the significance of what he was asking them to do: "By this everyone will know that you are my disciples, if you have love for one another" (John 13:34-35). Earlier in his ministry Jesus had also explained that the entire law of God is based on the two great commandments: love of God and love of neighbor (Matthew 22:37-40).

Paul recognized that loving one another—that is, obeying Jesus' new commandment—is the true measure and hallmark of a Christian. Knowing this, he urged the believers in Rome, "Owe no one anything except to love one another; for he who loves his neighbor has fulfilled the law" (Romans 13:8). And to the Galatians, confused about the ritual obligations of the law that the Judaizers had tried to lay on them like a heavy weight, he wrote, "Through love be servants of one another. The whole law is fulfilled in one word, 'You shall love your neighbor as yourself'" (Galatians 5:13-14). The "burdens" the Galatians were to bear were not those of the Mosaic Law, but those of loving their fellow church members—day in and day out, in good times and in bad.

Loving one another means helping each other bear the cares of daily life. That might be as simple as making a phone call to cheer up a friend who's feeling down. Or, more seriously, it might mean helping a neighbor recuperating from surgery by caring for her children or shopping for groceries.

Perhaps the burden we are to bear is to respond lovingly when we discover someone close to us has made a serious mistake or even committed a grave sin. Maybe it is to forgive someone who has hurt us—even if that person is unaware of the pain he or she has caused. It can be so easy to become angry, to gossip about that person to someone else, or even to break off the relationship. And yet, it is by sowing the seeds of love and mercy that we can reap a harvest of the Spirit. So, "as we have opportunity, let us do good to all" (Galatians 6:10).

"Lord Jesus, show me how I can fulfill your law of love today and help others to bear the burdens of life."

Galatians 6:11-18

[11]   See with what large letters I am writing to you with my own hand. [12] It is those who want to make a good showing in the flesh that would compel you to be circumcised, and only in order that they may not be persecuted for the cross of Christ. [13] For even those who receive circumcision do not themselves keep the law, but they desire to have you circumcised that they may glory in your flesh. [14] But far be it from me to glory except in the cross of our Lord Jesus Christ, by which the world has been crucified to me, and I to the world. [15] For neither circumcision counts for anything, nor uncircumcision, but a new creation. [16] Peace and mercy be upon all who walk by this rule, upon the Israel of God.

[17]   Henceforth let no man trouble me; for I bear on my body the marks of Jesus.

[18]   The grace of our Lord Jesus Christ be with your spirit, brethren. Amen.

The following words, commenting on this passage from St. Paul, are taken from a sermon by St. Theodore the Studite (759-826):

How precious the gift of the cross, how splendid to contemplate! . . . This was the tree on which Christ, like a king on a chariot, destroyed the devil, the Lord of death, and freed the human race from his tyranny. This was the tree upon which the Lord, like a brave warrior wounded in hands, feet and side, healed the wounds of sin that the evil serpent had inflicted on our nature. . . .

What an astonishing transformation! That death should become life, that decay should become immortality, that shame should become glory! Well might Paul exclaim: *Far be it from me to glory except in the cross of our Lord Jesus Christ, by which the world has been crucified to me, and I to the world!* The supreme wisdom that flowered on the cross has shown the folly of worldly wisdom's pride. The knowledge of all good, which is the fruit of the cross, has cut away the shoots of wickedness.

The wonders accomplished through this tree were foreshadowed clearly by the mere types and figures that existed in the past. Meditate on these, if you are eager to learn. Was it not the wood of a tree that enabled Noah, at God's command, to escape the destruction of the flood together with his sons, his wife, his sons' wives and every kind of animal? And surely the rod of Moses prefigured the cross when it changed water into blood, swallowed up the false serpents of Pharaoh's magicians, divided the sea at one stroke and then restored the waters to their normal course, drowning the enemy and saving God's own people. Aaron's rod, which blossomed in one day in proof of his true priesthood, was another figure of the cross, and did not Abraham foreshadow the cross when he bound his son Isaac and placed him on the pile of wood?

By the cross death was slain and Adam was restored to life. The cross is the glory of all the apostles, the crown of the martyrs, the sanctification of the saints. By the cross we put on Christ and cast aside our former self. By the cross we, the sheep of Christ, have been gathered into one flock, destined for the sheepfolds of heaven.

"Lord Jesus, open my eyes to see the glory of your cross. Fill me with wonder at the salvation and new life you won for me through your death. May I boast only in your cross!"

The New Testament
Devotional Commentary Series From
The Word Among Us Press

Matthew: A Devotional Commentary
Mark: A Devotional Commentary
Luke: A Devotional Commentary
John: A Devotional Commentary
Acts: A Devotional Commentary
Leo Zanchettin, General Editor

Enjoy praying through the New Testament with commentaries that include each passage of Scripture with a faith-filled meditation.

Also from The Word Among Us Press:
The Wisdom Series

Love Songs: Wisdom from Saint Bernard of Clairvaux
Live Jesus! Wisdom from Saints Francis de Sales and Jane de Chantal
A Radical Love: Wisdom from Dorothy Day
My Heart Speaks: Wisdom from Pope John XXIII
Welcoming the New Millennium: Wisdom from Pope John II
Touching the Risen Christ: Wisdom from The Fathers
Walking with the Father: Wisdom from Brother Lawrence
Hold Fast to God: Wisdom from The Early Church
Even unto Death: Wisdom from Modern Martyrs

These popular books include short biographies of the authors and selections from their writings grouped around themes such as prayer, forgiveness, and mercy.

To Order call 1-800-775-9673
or order online at www.wau.org